Melissa,

Thank you for
dedication and
course. I hope
text helpful
Controllah Gabi          07/12/2~

C000125269

# The Dissertation
## A Guide for Social Sciences

For Students, Dissertation Supervisors and Lecturers

CONTROLLAH GABI PhD
University Centre, Trafford College Group, UK

JOSEPHINE GABI PhD
Manchester Metropolitan University, UK

Published by
Confluence Information Services
83 Ducie Street
Manchester  M1 2JQ
England
UK

First published in the United Kingdom 2018

---

# DEDICATION

To our son
Prince Controllah Junior

# CONTENTS

ACKNOWLEDGMENTS x

1 INTRODUCTION TO THE DISSERTATION 1

    1.1 Overview 1

    1.2 What is the purpose of the dissertation? 1

    1.3 What are the key elements of a dissertation? 2

    1.4 What does it involve? 7

    1.5 What does it take to succeed? 10

    1.6 Summary 11

2 THE RESEARCH PROCESS 13

    2.1 Overview 13

    2.2 Choosing the best research topic 13

    2.3 Literature search and literature survey 16

    2.4 Data collection methodology decisions 17

    2.5 Data analysis 19

    2.6 Discussion 19

    2.7 Write-up considerations 20

    2.8 Summary 21

3 THE RESEARCH PROPOSAL 23

    3.1 Overview 23

    3.2 What is a research proposal? 24

    3.3 Purpose of a research proposal 24

    3.4 Structure and key content of a research proposal 25

    3.5 Summary 32

4 REVIEWING THE LITERATURE 33

    4.1 Overview 33

    4.2 What is a Literature Review? 34

4.3 The significance of a literature review    34

4.4 Key considerations    34

4.5 Searching for and surveying new literature    35

4.6 Identify key relevant themes    36

4.7 Structuring your literature review    37

4.8 Summary    42

5 DATA COLLECTION METHODS AND METHODOLOGIES    43

5.1 Overview    43

5.2 What are methods and what are methodologies?    43

5.3 Qualitative research methods    44

5.4 Quantitative research methods    62

5.5 Mixed-methods research    69

5.6 Research paradigms: What they are and their place    70

5.7 Summary    75

6 SOUNDNESS: VALIDITY, RELIABILITY, QUALITATIVE CRITERIA    77

6.1 Overview    77

6.2 Validity    77

6.3 Reliability    82

6.4 Alternative qualitative criteria    83

6.5 Triangulation    84

6.6 Ontology and epistemology    85

6.7 Consistency: Keeping harmony within the study    88

6.8 Summary    89

7 ETHICAL CONSIDERATIONS    91

7.1 Overview    91

7.2 What are ethics?    92

7.3 Social research ethical principles    100

7.4 Summary                                                      102

8 DATA ANALYSIS METHODS AND METHODOLOGIES        105

8.1 Overview                                                     105

8.2 Qualitative data analysis approaches                         107

8.3 Quantitative data analysis                                   115

8.4 Integrative analysis                                         119

8.5 Presenting your findings                                     120

8.6 Interpretation questionability                               122

8.7 Writing the conclusion                                       123

8.8 Self-reflexivity                                             125

8.9 Summary                                                      126

9 DISCUSSING FINDINGS AND USING EVIDENCE            129

9.1 Overview                                                     129

9.2 Interpreting the significance of findings                    129

9.3 Describing the significance of findings                      135

9.4 Explaining new insights                                      136

9.5 Summary                                                      138

10 IMPLICATIONS FOR PRACTICE, RECOMMENDATIONS FOR
FURTHER RESEARCH AND CONCLUSIONS                    139

10.1 Overview                                                    139

10.2 Purpose of the final chapter                                139

10.3 Being reflexive                                             142

10.4 Implications of findings to understanding of the subject    143

10.5 Summary                                                     144

11 THE ABSTRACT and Appendices                      145

11.1 Overview                                                    145

11.2 The abstract                                                145

| | |
|---|---|
| 11.3 Appendices | 146 |
| 11.4 Summary | 147 |
| GLOSSARY | 149 |
| References | 159 |
| Index | 165 |
| ABOUT THE AUTHORS | 171 |

# ACKNOWLEDGMENTS

Our students, past and present
Insightful. Humorous. Talented.
Our fellow educationists
Consistently, persistently enlightening the world.

# 1 INTRODUCTION TO THE DISSERTATION

## 1.1 Overview

The dissertation forms a critical component of most social sciences degrees. We view it as the unification part of a degree which brings together skills, knowledge and interests generated in a range of subjects on the course. In part, that is why this component of degree assessment tends to come in the final year of the degree programme. Additionally, its weighting in degree credits is usually double that of other programme modules, underscoring its importance in the overall scheme of the course. Thus, the wordage of the dissertation, depending on the nature of course, is relatively much higher.

The purpose of this chapter is to give you an overview of the expectations, content, structure and process of the dissertation component. Among other things, the chapter will treat key terms students need to be aware of, alongside what a dissertation in the social sciences context is. There will also be guidance on the general purpose of the dissertation component on a degree programme. Next will be an explanation of the key elements of a dissertation student's need to be aware of, what these involve and what it takes to enjoy and succeed in the dissertation process. Here we advisedly attach particular importance to the process for one specific reason – if you get the process right, the outcome will likely be a positive one.

## 1.2 What is the purpose of the dissertation?

The dissertation is probably the most complex comprehensive independently produced piece of work you will work on as a student. Among many purposes, the primary aim of the dissertation as an assessment strategy is to give the student an opportunity to demonstrate their ability to carry out a small-scale project primarily involving research planning, literature review, research instrument design, data collection and analysis and writing up. For the student, it is an opportunity to explore in some depth a topic, or an aspect of a topic, they wish to find out more about and draw insights from in an ethical manner. Because this project is mostly self-directed, it is reasonable to hope that the student also enjoys the dissertation process, especially as it is a drawn-out technically taxing process. If the student does not enjoy the process, it becomes harder and more mechanical, undertaken out of obligation rather than out of interest. Therefore, interest in the subject or topic, self-confidence and a mutually positive working relationship with the dissertation supervisor will likely have a positive impact on the student's experience of the dissertation project experience.

## 1.3 What are the key elements of a dissertation?

The composition of a dissertation may vary by academic institution or department and degree programme. Still, there are common constituent elements of a good dissertation. These include an abstract, introduction, literature review, methods and methodologies, data analysis, discussion and recommendations and conclusions. It is important, however, to note that the wording and organisation of these elements may be different across programmes and universities. Even so, what is important is noting the content as expectations regarding a sound dissertation are generally similar. Below is a descriptive overview of each element.

### 1.3.1 Abstract

The purpose of the dissertation abstract is to give the reader an overview of the dissertation which is sufficient enough to inform them about the study, including its key findings, so they may decide if the work is something they would be interested in reading before they commit much time to it. Therefore, a good abstract is supposed to stand alone, independent of the dissertation, even though it is usually physically bound to the dissertation. In essence, it must – on its own – provide sufficient overview information on the dissertation. Primarily,

2

therefore, a sufficient abstract will describe the research focus, the sample, methods and methodologies used and key findings. Because an academic abstract is usually no longer than 500 words, it is of paramount importance that it is written succinctly. We strongly recommend that you follow your degree wordage stipulation.

## 1.3.2 Introduction

The introduction chapter is important as it provides the background to the dissertation. While academic departments may be prescriptive on what they expect in the introduction chapter, there are common features of a sound dissertation introduction chapter. These include **overview**, **purpose**, **problem** and **structure** (*OPPS*).

The *overview* part of the introduction chapter serves a number of important purposes. In the main, it offers snapshot background to the research topic. The background can be a historical perspective on the topic or subject.

To give the reader a sense of the aim of the work, the *purpose* aspect spells out the research focus, research questions and/or aims and rationale. A good dissertation must be narrowed down to a specific, determinable focal point. This must be declared at the onset in order to make it easy for the reader to understand the work. For consistency, this declared focal point must then be built on throughout the work. We also recommend that research questions your work seeks to answer are included to enhance the purpose of the study.

Building on the outlined purpose, the *statement of the problem* explains in sufficient and definite detail what it is that your dissertation seeks to either improve on, solve, add to, eliminate or tackle a troubling question in key literature or existing practice. This can always reflectively be revisited in the conclusions in light of emerging findings.

Finally, the *structure* section of the introduction chapter seeks to signpost the reader as to how the dissertation is organised. It is good academic practice to enable the reader to anticipate the structure of, and therefore logically mentally prepare for, the sequencing of the dissertation. So, ensure that your signposting is consistent with, or accurately reflective of, the actual structure of the work.

### 1.3.3 Literature review

Before we look at what it is that you are expected to do in your literature review, it is important to consider what a literature review is. Literature refers to all scholarly work on the topic or in the area of study. This work comprises the published and unpublished body, including but not limited to, books, journals, theses, research reports, videos and conference proceedings. In simple terms, other words for the word review are *appraise*, *evaluate*, *assess*, *examine*, *analyse* or *criticise*. Therefore, a literature review can be described as a critical appraisal, evaluation, assessment, examination, analysis or critique of a major published and unpublished body of knowledge on a topic or field of enquiry.

The literature review is a key component of the dissertation. In it you critically consider current knowledge, and how this knowledge has been generated, on the topic you wish to research. Here it is important to bear in mind that almost every topic or line of enquiry has been previously studied and, therefore, what your own research is doing is building on or extending this knowledge. So, your review of the literature aims to find out what other researchers or authors say, both in published and unpublished work, on the subject or topic you are interested in. Another aspect the literature review deals with is how others have researched the topic. In this regard, you are looking for ideas on key research elements like methods utilised, how these methods have been used, sampling, research instruments, ethical issues and other potential topic problems and key findings and their implications. In the process, you should also critically analyse all literature under review.

### 1.3.4 Methods and methodologies

The methods and methodologies chapter deals with research techniques and how these techniques have been used in your study. In other words, methods are *what* has been done and methodologies are *how* the methods have been used. Therefore, methods address specific research *actions* while methodologies have to do with the *process*. It is also important to remember that everything you have done and every research instrument you have used in your research must be justified.

So, in the methods and methodologies chapter, you must include three key components: *what*, *how* and *why*. The *what* are the methods and instruments. The *how* are the processes or procedures followed in the use of the methods and instruments. The *why* are the justifications or reasons for the *what* and the *how*. You must justify the methods and the methodologies. You can take the methods and methodologies to be a six-question iteration:

1. What did you do?
2. How did you do what you did?
3. Why did you do what you did the way you did it?
4. What did you use to do what you did?
5. How did you use what you used to do what you did?
6. Why did you use what you used the way you used it?

## 1.3.5 Findings and analysis

The findings and analysis chapter focuses on the outcomes of your research. For it to be effective, this chapter must be written in a systematic manner. To achieve this, there is need for you to logically look at patterns in your data and what possible meanings these data may carry in the context of your work and field of study. A lot of time must be devoted to exploring a range of often competing lines of enquiry and interrogating your findings from a range of perspectives. If done properly, your findings and analysis will produce multiple possible plausible interpretations. Hence the recommendation we make when it comes to findings and analysis is that you interrogate your data rigorously and draw insights.

Since most data is likely to present the challenge of excessive output, it is important that you are focused in your undertaking. The best strategy would be to reconsider your research questions or research aims you will have set at the beginning of your study. This narrows down your analyses to only what your study is interested in. Doing this will help you identify, classify and group your data according to their relevance to your research questions during which or after which links and patterns – again in relation to research questions or research aims – are identified.

## 1.3.6 Discussion

Different researchers approach this differently. Some combine discussion with findings and analysis while others separate their discussion chapter from findings and analysis. Either way, it is still paramount that you know what a sound discussion of findings entails. A good discussion of findings makes sense of the outcomes in light of existing literature on the subject. It considers similarities to and differences from findings from similar studies. In light of this, the discussion also attempts to address what these findings, therefore, mean.

Throughout, always bear in mind the context of your study. In essence, the discussion must answer the following questions:

1. What do these findings mean in context?
2. What do the findings confirm?
3. What do the findings contradict?
4. How different are the findings from those of previous studies?
5. What is new from the findings?
6. What do the findings mean for the topic/ field and practice?

## 1.3.7 Recommendations and conclusions

It is also expected that a good research project will have some future impact on research and practice. Therefore, you need to identify the possible impact of your study on future research in the field and on practice. In keeping, you need to come up with suggestions for further study and outline implications for practice. This will likely be your work's contribution to knowledge and practice.

In comparison to other chapters, this chapter tends to be briefer and more descriptive. There is very little explanation or detailed elaboration as this will have been done elsewhere in the dissertation already. Still, it must make sense and should be consistent with your findings, analysis and discussion.

Following up on recommendations, and consistent with your dissertation's major findings, there is need to draw conclusions from your study. This is where you tie everything up together so that it collectively makes sense. The question you will be addressing here is: All things considered, what are the key take-aways from my study?

Here there is no hard and fast rule on the content, but you may want to consider your research globally in roughly three parts:

1. Conclusions regarding key findings.
2. Conclusions regarding research process.
3. Conclusions regarding the future of study in the area.

Whichever direction you opt to take, ensure your conclusions are contextualised within the study, balanced and instructive. Still, do remember that this section should be brief and to the point. Avoid labouring your points.

## 1.4 What does it involve?

In brief, carrying out a degree research project involves identifying a topic of interest, surveying the literature on the topic for ideas and opportunities for research, planning, consulting, undertaking, organising, analysis and writing. We give brief descriptions of each of these below.

As much as it appears simple, identifying a topic of interest is an important step towards a successful research endeavour. It requires much careful consideration. Among other important things, it is key that you select a topic you are confident tackling. This can be on either personal, professional or academic interest. At the same time, it should be a topic you think you will also learn something new from, rather than a topic you think you will show off what you know already. If you know it already, there is no value in researching it! Another consideration here should be whether this topic is doable with your skillset and supervisor support available. For example, if neither you nor supervisor support available are proficient in quantitative methodologies it would be futile to carry out a study of the nature as the chances of getting it wrong are high. Remember, you aspire to make a contribution to knowledge, and this knowledge must be meaningful. Some topics are consistent with certain methodologies while others may be best studied using another set of methodologies.

Even when you have made up your mind on what topic to do your research on, surveying the literature still remains an important task. This is the initial reading you carry out in order to have an idea what other researchers have done in the field, what instruments they have used, how they have done the research, what their findings were and recommendations they put forward. Thus, at the onset, you will have

– for example – an impression of what the research process will likely take, if you need to design your own instruments or would like to consider using what is already there with a few adaptations, if it suits your research focus. Perhaps more importantly, surveying the literature will give you an indication of whether there is enough material published to meaningfully use in your study. If very little has been published, you may find it a challenge to carry out your study as sound research is usually built on sound literature. This early into your research journey, as a student, you may struggle to determine why there seems to be very little published in an area you may personally consider very important. Could it be that it is not considered as important by other researchers? You may end up having very little to work off, thereby putting you at a disadvantage relative to other students on your programme. In this case, we would recommend that you consult your dissertation supervisor for direction. They may suggest a slight change in direction before it is too late, or they may recommend a complete change in research topic. Frustrating as this may feel, you would rather this decision is made early, before you commit too much time and effort into a pathway with far too many hurdles to navigate successfully.

Say you are now happy with your topic and are confident it is doable with your skillset, available supervisor support and within the set timeframe, planning is still very important. We hope you have heard the adage: Failing to plan is planning to fail. When a module is as major as the dissertation, succeeding in it will give you big gains as, in most cases, dissertations have double the number of credits in other modules. Therefore, succeeding in your dissertation is double success relative to other modules on your course. Unfortunately, the converse is also true. Failing in a double-credit module doubles the loss you make relative to other modules. So, planning is a good step towards achieving this major success in your dissertation. Draw up a plan of what needs to be done when and what your key indicators of success will be for each stage. Because it is a long, drawn out project, it is easy to think you have a lot of time when that is not the case. It is also easy to go off-track and not realise it until it is too late to take corrective action. Draw up a plan and share it with your supervisor for advice. More importantly, try your best to stick to that plan. Ticking activities off your plan as you progress will give you further impetus towards achieving your overall goal of completing your project. Also remember to leave ample editing and proofreading time at the end before the work is submitted.

No matter how confident you are or how competent you think you are, it is of absolute importance that you consult your supervisor consistently throughout your journey. After all, you are paying to obtain this support, so why should you not access it? In most cases, you will have suitably qualified and experienced research supervisors to provide you with the necessary guidance. They will assist, question and sometimes challenge your work, processes and decisions. At times they will correct errors that may weaken the integrity of your work. All this is before you make the final submission. This is called formative assessment which, in simple terms, means assessment intended to enhance learning. It is better for your work to be critiqued while there is still an opportunity to do something about it than after the final submission has been made.

You may have the best research idea, an exceptional plan, impeccable literature to work with and the most highly-qualified research supervisor. Added to this, you may be the best student to ever do your course. All this will count for nothing if you do not actually do the work. The evidence of excellence is in doing the work to the best of your ability, making the most of available supervisor support and resources. Undertaking the research is of absolute importance, and undertaking it the right way is of even greater absolute importance. We always tell our students that you do not submit ideas in their abstract; you submit soundly completed work! We do not mark abstract ideas. We mark work! So, you will need to put all those good ideas you have to use. Put your plan into action. To many ideas there is no end, but to good deeds there is a good end.

Doing is good. Doing it right is divine. To get the dissertation process right, you need to organise every aspect of your dissertation endeavour. Organising includes, inter alia, putting your research processes in order, ensuring you gather all necessary resources and use them effectively, having and following a research timetable, gaining access into research settings and using it, collecting, collating and analysing data and writing up. Being organised enables you to be systematic in your approach to and conduct of your work. It is not enough to do your dissertation work. You need to do it right. Organising and being organised is at the core of getting it right.

In addition to elements we have covered above, consistent critical analysis will strengthen the integrity of your dissertation. This involves making links or connections, establishing patterns, identifying contradictions, making comparisons, corroborating and drawing inferences or conclusions. Questioning is also a critical component of analysis.

So, you are on track. Yes, you have read the relevant literature. Yes, you have designed the research instruments. Yes, you may even have collected the data and analysed it. You still need to write the dissertation. Now, as you will rightly guess, there is no single dominant approach to carrying out the writing. However, most successful students in dissertations tend to start their writing early. Components like the literature review can be written while you collect your data. Of course, you can always go back to the chapter to make minor amendments, if this is necessary. Do your writing progressively. Most higher education institutions give students opportunities to send their draft chapters to supervisors for formative feedback. If your institution does this, we advise you make the most of these opportunities. From our experience, students who tend to do well are those who engage with the supervision process systematically. This also helps keeps you on track with your writing.

## 1.5 What does it take to succeed?

Succeeding in your dissertation takes a combination of skill, ambition, endeavour, support, focus and being practical. You need to have the relevant skillset to carry out the research of the nature you choose to undertake. Even with the right skills, you still need the ambition to do something you feel is unique, something that is identifiable to you, an original piece of work. It may be similar to other work in some respects, but there must be aspects you still identify as reflective of your original effort. Due to the dissertation project being lengthy and somewhat drawn out, you must demonstrate much endeavour and persistence to see it through. You will not always feel consistent energy levels during the course of this project. At the back of your mind, remember that the role of the dissertation supervisor in giving formative feedback is that of a critical friend – one who tells you inconvenient truths for your benefit. Sometimes you may receive feedback you may consider discouraging. At other times, you may feel like you cannot do it. In all instances, it is important to keep going. Talk to other students. Talk to your dissertation supervisor. Remain tenacious, pressing towards your goal, drawing from multiple reservoirs of strength, particularly strategic networks of support available. Finally, being practical or pragmatic is that tendency to just get things done in whatever circumstances you may find yourself confronted with. This is called direct action, realising that, unless you do it, work will not do itself – neither will someone else do it in your stead.

## 1.6 Summary

In this chapter we have provided an overview of the dissertation process. We, therefore, hope that now you have a general idea of what a dissertation is, what the project involves and what it takes to succeed. Building on this foundation, our aim in the following chapters is give you the necessary grounding in the content and processes of an undergraduate social sciences dissertation module. While we set out to provide the most important advice and guidance, we are mindful of the likelihood that you probably have too busy a degree workload to be concerned with the detail of what you probably do not need at this level. Thus, we will do our best to present this book as a sourcebook which only contains what you need to succeed in your dissertation at degree level, something you can use as a reference book or manual.

# 2 THE RESEARCH PROCESS

## 2.1 Overview

As in most academic work, a rigorous, well-thought-out process forms a good basis for a positive outcome. To do well in your dissertation, you need to pay particular attention to doing it well. By *doing it well* we refer to getting the process right, in a systematic academic way. Far too many times, students expend their effort by obsessing with what grade they will get, rather than directing their energy towards what it is they need to do to meet the requirements for a sound research project. Focus should be on the *process*. The grade is an outcome of the *process*, so it will take care of itself while you take care of the *process*.

In this chapter, we will go through the fundamentals of a sound research process. We will take you through the key decisions you will have to make at various points of your dissertation project. Primarily, we will explain options available, what to consider in choosing the best option and how you may justify these decisions. We will start with the key decision of when and how to choose the best research topic. This will be followed by an elucidation of literature search and literature survey decision issues. After this, we will go through data collection methodology decisions. This will include, among other important things, choice of sample, gaining access, ethical considerations, timing and duration. We will also look at data analysis, discussion and write-up considerations.

## 2.2 Choosing the best research topic

We do not wish to prescribe a definitive way in which you ought to choose your research topic. We are conscious that research topic selection is influenced by a plethora of factors, far too complex to unpick. Yet our experience persuades us that most undergraduate students choose their topics from modules they will have covered. Of course, the underlying reasons for choosing a particular topic could well be either personal, academic or professional. Even so, almost all of our students' research topics still have been influenced by aspects they have learned in class. One of the major explanations for why these students are swayed towards topics covered in their lectures is that initial ideas will have been generated and some arguments tested during classroom engagement. Thus, at least for these students, working on an idea or concept that has – in some shape or form – been tested lowers the perceived risk of the largely untested, unknown or unfamiliar.

Different researchers prefer following different processes for selecting their research topics. One of the most effective processes involves starting with a broad area of interest and working down to a narrower, more focused topic. In this respect, we suggest following the stages below in which we are proposing working from the general to the particular, from the broad to the specific.

## 2.2.1 Stage 1: Identify a broad area you are interested in

You most probably have a general area of study in which you are interested. Some of our students, for example, have shown a general interest in inclusive education. Others have been interested in children's mental health and yet others have been keen on learning more on the effects of poverty. Now these areas are too broad to research on in a small research project in the limited timeframe available. That said, it is usually helpful as a starting point to have a broad area of research interest. It gives you the flexibility on the direction you want to take as you gather more information which influences your eventual decision.

## 2.2.2 Stage 2: Outline possible topics you are interested in

Under your broad area of interest, you need to then outline possible topics you are interested in for further examination. While the list will initially be long, we suggest that you keep it to a length you can meaningfully work with. As this is not the final list, do not focus on perfection too much at this stage. What is important, therefore, is not the purity of the grammar. Rather, at this stage you are looking at the rough ideas as part of the process to, hopefully, narrow down to a particular research focus. For instance, under poverty as a broad area, a student could consider the following as possible research topics:

- The impact of poverty on children's wellbeing
- Factors influencing child poverty
- The relationship between poverty and attainment among primary school children
- An evaluation of the effectiveness of government strategies for addressing child poverty in nursery settings

As you have probably noticed, some of these possible topics might require further tweaking until you are satisfied you can comfortably and confidently tackle the topic. There is a somewhat objective way in which you can do this, which is our proposed next step.

### 2.2.3 Stage 3: Objectively score these topics

Our guess is you will be passionate about all potential topics you will have identified in the first stage, otherwise they will not have made your list. But you will only be working on just one topic for your dissertation. So, you have to go through a potentially difficult process of eliminating some topics you will find hard to drop. One way of getting around which one of your many topics is the best is ask yourself how each of the topics would score if you were to assess individual candidate topic's strengths. Here is a list of possible research project plausibility and doability criteria on a scale of 1 (very weak) to 5 (very strong). Feel free and confident to modify at your discretion:

1. To what extent is the topic relevant to my degree?
2. Will the topic generate sufficient data for a dissertation of this magnitude and length?
3. Available literature to work with on the topic.
4. Access to a sufficient sample to conduct research on the topic.
5. Contextual ethical acceptability.
6. Doability of the research within the given timeframe.
7. Strength of the topic in enabling you to meet your dissertation assessment criteria.
8. Potential to contribute to knowledge, policy and/ or practice.
9. Your competence and confidence in undertaking research on the topic area and appropriate methods and methodologies.

10. Availability of sufficient supervision expertise in the topic.

Calculate totals of each of your topics' scores and choose the highest scoring. It is possible you may want to go for the topic scoring second for reasons personal to you, but at least you will have been somewhat systematic in your approach. All factors considered, select the one you are happiest with in accordance with the scores. But picking a topic scoring last in your own assessment of topics would be risky.

Another way to tackle the 'too hard to drop' topic dilemma would be selecting what you consider the strongest and converting the rest to research questions. Because this is somewhat complex, we suggest you refer to the section dealing with formulating research questions as research questions are generally narrower and more focused than research topics. It is also worth checking with your dissertation supervisor for further guidance as different supervisors have different expectations on almost everything.

## 2.3 Literature search and literature survey

Knowing *where* to search is as important as knowing *what* to search. Also, of great importance is knowing *how* to search. These aspects are explored in greater detail in chapter 4. What we consider in this section, however, are the decision points of literature searching and literature surveying.

### 2.3.1 Working with what you know

We make the assumption that you will most likely have chosen a research topic from modules or units you will have covered during the course of your study so far. That being the case, you will, therefore have received some valuable feedback from your lecturers on such things as the quality and use of sources to support your arguments. Now, this is good starting point as opposed to starting from scratch, with nothing to work with. You will have some potentially good sources to get you started. Working with the familiar is good for your confidence and sense of direction. But it is important, however, to note that this is only a starting point. There still is considerably more work to be done to enhance the quality and integrity of your dissertation. This is especially so for a number of reasons. Key among these factors is likelihood that a lot more literature will have been generated since that feedback was given. Additionally, you will also likely need to factor in improvement points marker(s) assessing the work in question will have put forward.

One pitfall you will need to avoid, especially when it comes to working with what you have used previously, is assuming that if your work was assessed as excellent in a certain assignment it will be considered excellent in a dissertation context. While it may still be considered excellent, it is highly unusual that this is the case. There are two main reasons why what you already have may be assessed differently if not adapted to the dissertation context. From our experience, students bringing work from level 5 (second year of the undergraduate degree) to level 6 (third year of the undergraduate degree), for example, are frustrated when they are advised to improve on the work. The thinking is simple, level 6 standards are generally higher and, therefore, more stringent than level 5. Another reason why what you already have may not be good enough in its current state is that the module context is different and, therefore, expectations will likely differ. Accordingly, there is every chance that your existing literature should only be considered a platform on which to build, as opposed to being a finished product that is readily transferrable to the dissertation without adaptations. An additional influence on why what you already have may also need adapting is that you will also have progressed in your thinking since you last used the work in question and, thus, you will want the work to also reflect the progress you will have made or changes in some of the positions you will have held previously on a subject covered by that work. Whatever the case may be, always remember that knowledge and its pursuit are in constant evolution, not fixity.

## 2.4 Data collection methodology decisions

There are many data collection methods and methodology decisions you ought to make right from the start. Ultimately, it is the soundness of your methods and methodologies which will have a strong bearing on the integrity of your work, primarily its reliability and validity. You have probably heard that your dissertation lives or dies on its methods and methodologies. While there is an element of exaggeration in this notion, the importance of methods and methodology to the architecture of your dissertation cannot be emphasised enough.

Key methodology decisions have to do with data collection methods, related data collection instruments, how these instruments will be used and suitability or appropriateness of these instruments to the type and size of sample of participants. Related to this, the choice of sample is, therefore, important. There are two considerations you will need to make in this regard. Either there will be need for you to adapt your data collection instruments to your sample. For example, simplifying an existing questionnaire to make it accessible or understandable to children. Alternatively, you could target a sample which will be able to make sense of your data collection instruments or methodologies. Certain interviews, for instance, will suit certain age groups. On the same wavelength, people to whom English is a second language may find focus groups conducted in English inaccessible.

Without access to participant settings there is no research. Even though it sounds simple, access to your participants is critical to your ability to conduct the research. It would be catastrophic if you went ahead and started writing your literature review and designing your research instruments only to find out much later that you are unable to gain access into a setting in which you had intended to carry out your research. In light of this, it is critical that you negotiate and obtain access as soon as you are clear what kind of research you are going to conduct. Most settings require key information on your study to enable them to make sufficiently informed decisions on whether to grant you access. Mostly, this information includes – but is not limited to – research topic, aims, what the data collection will involve, timetable of the data collection, terms of participation and participant data protection considerations. Some of these issues will have been addressed at research ethics approval stage. Still, it is important that you provide sufficient enough information to settings in which you intend to carry out your research. Settings will vary in their requirements. However, it is still important that you are truthful and conduct yourself with utmost integrity as not only your reputation is at stake, but also your institution's.

## 2.5 Data analysis

There are contrasting perspectives on when data analysis methodology decisions should be made. That said, we envisage that an organised student will have an idea on the data analysis methods and methodologies they will use before they embark on data collection. Needless to say, certain data collection methods and methodologies lend themselves to certain data analysis methods and methodologies. Here key considerations are compatibility and consistency of approaches. On the other hand, some data collection approaches, for instance the grounded theory, require that data analysis begins during data collection. Thus, waiting until after data collection to determine your data analysis methods and methodologies is not a good idea since, in all probability, it will be too late to make such an important decision.

Another important point to consider is the consistency between, and compatibility of, data analysis approaches and data collection methods and methodologies. On this front, we recommend that qualitative data be analysed using qualitative analysis methodologies. Likewise, quantitative data should be analysed with quantitative data analysis methodologies. Regarding the specifics of the data analysis tradition you will employ, this must be largely based on what gives you the best possible return on your research questions.

## 2.6 Discussion

The discussion, as every other aspect we have so far considered, should be taken as a process comprising a number of deliberate stages. This approach, as opposed to arbitrariness, helps you arrive at a systematic discussion that is easy to follow for the reader and, for you, more manageable. It enables you to determine whether, and to what extent, your discussion sufficiently treats key findings relative to set research questions. Being systematic with your discussion, as a process, also enhances your works potential to address dissertation learning outcomes and assessment criteria.

The best way to approach your discussion is to start planning for it during the early stages of your data analysis – as early as during annotation and identification of data for consideration in in-depth analysis. At this stage you are asking questions regarding why the data you are identifying and/ or annotating is important, what possible explanations or reasons exist for why this identified data deserves further consideration and where this data stands in relation to existing literature. In this case, it is probable that you will note corroboration and contradiction with different pieces of literature. In addition, you also need to start thinking about how you are going to explain the corroborations and contradictions.

To enhance your discussion, there is further need for you to think, early on, what the key findings mean from a range of perspectives. For example, you need to contemplate what the key findings mean for theory, practice and/ or policy. Do not limit this to just the future. Rather, be holistic in your approach, looking at precedent (past), present and possible future. In respect of the future, we take the view that it can only be considered a possibility, not a certainty, because there are too many unknowns to be completely certain what the future implications for your findings will be. Therefore, it is academically prudent to always express caution in your writing about future implications of your key findings. As we have stated previously, there is need for you to be analytical when you draw possible meanings of your findings from emerging patterns and links between and within sometimes disparate chunks of data.

## 2.7 Write-up considerations

As we have proffered earlier, the eventual assessment of your work will be based on the submitted dissertation, which is the work you have written up. Until such a time as you have completed the write-up, your dissertation work is not yet done. You may have excellent ideas, rich data or great insights. As long as this is not on paper in the required dissertation format, all this counts for nothing. Similarly, a poorly written up dissertation will likely score lowly regardless of how well the data collection, collation and analysis is. You still need to present your work in keeping with the dissertation requirements of your institution or department.

During your planning stage, there are a number of important considerations you should take into account. These include wordage, nature of study, dissertation structure and your writing speed. Earlier we indicated that undergraduate dissertation wordage is significantly higher than that of other modules or units. Obviously, the amount of time you will take will, to a large extent, depend on the final word count of the dissertation. It is important, though, to bear in mind that this wordage usually refers to the main part of the dissertation, that is excluding references and appendices. So, it is of paramount importance that, in addition to wordage, you consider the size of your reference list and the length and structure of your appendices. All this takes time and needs to be planned for.

The nature of study has a significant bearing on how long it will take you to write up your dissertation. Some studies are mostly text-based while others will include a lot of diagrams. Depending on your computer proficiency, there will likely be a difference in the time taken to complete writing up different dissertation types. Therefore, you need to carefully plan for how long your type of dissertation will take to complete so that you do not rush it through in the end when you suddenly realise it cannot be meaningfully completed in time for submission. Equally important in your considerations are your dissertation structure and writing speed. If you generally take time to write, then you need to plan for more writing up time. As we have indicated earlier, you should also take into account the volume of your appendices when you plan your write-up. The more meticulous you are in your planning, the easier you will find it to implement your plan.

## 2.8 Summary

Research should be taken as a systematic process, as opposed to an arbitrary exercise. Knowing and considering what it takes to successfully complete the dissertation will help you, from the beginning, plan for the journey in an effective way. From data collection to writing up, carefully account for how much time and commitment the process will take. This will go a long way towards helping you confidently carry out the research project. Building on what we have covered in this chapter, chapter 3 looks at the research proposal/ plan in more depth.

# 3 THE RESEARCH PROPOSAL

## 3.1 Overview

A large proportion of social sciences degrees require students to submit a research proposal before they undertake their dissertation project. There are a number of reasons why this is, from both the student and the lecturer perspectives. For the student, a research proposal is an early opportunity to test their research idea against set criteria and to obtain valuable feedback on strengths and areas for improvement before they commit to the project. Apart from this, it also accords the student a chance to determine if their proposed research, and how it will be done, against an ethics test which will have to be satisfactorily passed before one can be allowed to proceed with their project. For the lecturer or supervisor, a research proposal is an early window through which they can make a determination of students' understanding of the research project and the range of topics being explored. This aids in equitable dissertation supervisor allocation. Additionally, lecturers or supervisors can also determine if all or certain students will need further assistance and direction prior to starting their project. This guidance and direction can be on any of a range of issues such as methodology consistency, topic and study feasibility and conceptual cogency. If an issue is common across a cohort of learners, lecturers will be able to ascertain what remedial action needs taking, such as group sessions on an aspect of research in class or identifying students needing one to one sessions on areas for further development prior to starting the research project. In a sense, from a lecturer's viewpoint, a research proposal – besides assessing student learning – can also be a tool with which they assess students' readiness for the dissertation project and, if not, identifying the nature and extent of support they need in order to enhance a reasonable level of readiness to carry out sound research appropriate for the study level.

As most research proposals at degree level tend to be summatively assessed as well, we think it is necessary to go through what a sound research proposal is and should contain. We also endeavour to cover common expectations for an effective, hence successful, academic research proposal. Therefore, in this chapter, we cover purpose, ideal content and structure of what can be considered a good research proposal. To begin with, we explore some definitions of a project proposal. We then proceed to discuss some key goals or purpose of a research proposal at undergraduate level. Next, we go through the key components of a sound research proposal. In the conclusion, we summarise this chapter and give a brief preview of the following chapter.

## 3.2 What is a research proposal?

There is no agreed-on universal definition of a research proposal. In that lack of consensus, however, there are certain features common across most definitions given in dominant literature on academic enquiry. We attempt to condense these features into a single, easy-to-understand definition. A research proposal is a brief outline of an intended empirical enquiry comprising an overview of current dominant discourses and debate on the topic, methods and methodologies to be used, proposed timeframe and how the proposed research is envisaged to contribute to the existing knowledge body on the chosen topic.

## 3.3 Purpose of a research proposal

A research proposal serves multiple purposes, depending on level of study and set learning outcomes. Besides the obvious summative assessment function, an academic research proposal helps you get your mind focused on what exactly you want to study for your research project, how, why and for how long. It is also a chance for you to establish if you are up to the topic you would like to focus on and if this is achievable in the available timeframe. It further prepares you in the sense that you start thinking about your topic in a more logical way than you do when exploring the topic in flimsy and somewhat abstract terms.

## 3.4 Structure and key content of a research proposal

The University of Birmingham (2018) offers a useful list of core content of a research proposal we wish to adopt for this section as it is, in our view, easy to use. Moreover, the list is consistent with the general research proposal expectations on most programmes. Typically, research proposals ought to include a proposed or working topic, an abstract, background or context of the research – which is mostly grounded in the main body of literature, research aim and/ or research questions, research methods, ethical considerations and significance of the proposed research.

### 3.4.1 Working topic of proposed research

As the wording suggests, the working topic of your proposed study is a snapshot of what your proposed enquiry is about. Its purpose is to give the reader an idea of what your intended study covers. As this is still just a proposal, there is always a possibility that this topic may change during the lifecycle of the study, should you then go on to implement the proposal. Even so, though you are still at the proposal stage of your research, there remains a strong need to take some care in arriving at your tentative research topic.

In a sense, the research topic or title can be characterised as a descriptive label of the investigation. Conceiving the research topic as a label is helpful in that it is instructive as to how you may approach this seemingly rudimentary task. In general, labels are useful for locating, signposting and sorting. In this regard, good labels make it easy for the audience to have an initial understanding of the type of product and identifying the product – as the label makes the product stand out. For those handling many different products, labels serve an important function of enabling these handlers to sort the products by subject, for example. Similarly, a good research topic should enable others to easily locate, identify and file the research proposal logically.

Pithiness is another important characteristic of a sound research topic. It is noteworthy that there appears to be no consensus in empirical enquiry, even in social sciences, on what can be considered an ideal research topic length. With this in mind, we believe that a good research topic must be brief enough to be understood without the need to re-read and long enough to give the reader an idea what the study is about. There is no need to say in more words what can be expressed in less. Brevity is always key. Just the main idea or ideas of your research suffice in the topic. There will be opportunities to provide detail in the body of the proposal. In tandem, the University of Southern California (2018: online) submits that a research topic is sound when it is expressed in the "fewest possible words needed to adequately describe the content and/ or aim" of the proposed research project.

### 3.4.2 Abstract

An abstract is a standalone overview of your research. Usually, this is presented in a single paragraph of between 100 and 300 words – but you need to check your course requirements on abstract wordage as there may be some variance between institutions and departments. That said, expectations on content and structure are principally consistent. Unlike the dissertation abstract, however, a research proposal abstract is customarily written in the future tense mainly because the research has not yet been conducted. Another dissimilarity with a dissertation abstract is that the research proposal abstract will not include findings since there are no research results yet. So, let us consider what should be in a research proposal abstract.

A research proposal abstract should describe the intended research project's aim, why this project will be carried out, what problem the study seeks to address or the broad question it intends to tackle and a description of the methods that will be employed in the study. Depending on the wordage of the abstract, you may add information about who your intended participants are or the setting in which the study will be conducted.

### 3.4.3 Research background

As mentioned earlier, the background of your proposed enquiry is mostly, if not exclusively, grounded in the literature. Again, this ought to be brief, in comparison to the literature review of the dissertation. This section of the research proposal is intended to provide context to your intended study. It serves to locate your study within the context of the existing body of knowledge. What is addressed in this section is a range of issues, but central to the content of this section is addressing the main question regarding what is currently known on the topic. To address this question, we advise that the section considers the key debates, propositions and perceived gaps or limitations in what is known on the topic.

The research background also gives the reader of your proposal an indication of your fluency in the subject you intend to research at the time of writing. The thinking behind this is that for you to do your research in a sufficiently rigorous and erudite way, you must have a solid basis informing your decision to pursue the study you are proposing to conduct. Thus, in this section you demonstrate your founding knowledge of the topic, particularly key debates, conceptual frameworks and limitations and/ or gaps in the literature. This will then give you an opportunity to argue why, in light of the literature, you think your proposed research is timely and addresses an important issue in the field. You are addressing the question to do with in what way, and to what extent, you consider your proposed enquiry to be significant. This can be addressed at two levels – academic and/ or professional. There are also further levels that can be argued effectively, for instance social and political strands. As long as you can reasonably argue your point for why and how your study makes a meaningful contribution to the existing body of knowledge and, therefore, worth doing, you should have the confidence that your research stands a decent chance of being accepted as a worthy endeavour.

It is further highly likely that your work will be building on another researcher's work which already exists in the body of knowledge. If this is the case, it is good ethical and academic practice to acknowledge this work in the context of the general body of literature you will be briefly reviewing. For example, a researcher may have studied resilience among primary-school aged pupils, and you wish to use this work to shape your own on resilience among nursery children. There is nothing wrong with extending that foundational study so that what was learned can be tested in a new context, although you may decide to adapt similar research methods and methodologies and instruments to your proposed work. Alternatively, you could argue for using different methods and methodologies to those employed in the preceding work for any specified academic reasons. You are still conducting your research in the context of existing work. What is important here is remembering that very rarely does empirical work occur in an academic vacuum. Almost always, there is context, and the burden is on you to demonstrate that you are aware of it.

### 3.4.4 Research aim(s) and research questions

Positions on which of research aims and research questions to include in the research proposal vary. One view is that you include both, and yet another is that you provide one or the other. There is, however, one firm position that you must spell out your research question, whether or not you decide to include your research aim(s). Our recommendation is that you must include research questions in your research proposal. But, first, let us consider what research aims and research questions are and their purpose in a research proposal.

Research aims are a set of broad statements of intent in relation to a proposed enquiry. They spell out what the study intends to ultimately achieve upon completion. In them, if properly drawn up, one can see what the focus of the study is and, hence, its parameters. For the researcher, research aims – thus – are a guide for the scope or boundaries, so to speak, of the intended study. From an assessment position, research aims enable whoever is appraising the proposal determine the achievability of what the proposer of the study is putting forward, all key factors considered. Beyond the research proposal stage, research aims serve an important purpose to the research as they are a form of a performance indicator – a means through which the researcher can self-assess, that is whether they achieved what they set out to achieve through their research. Accordingly, it is apparent why research aims can be considered important as early as the research proposal stage. In relatively small studies like dissertation enquiries, one research aim can suffice. Although you can have two or three, too many research aims can be considered infeasible in a set timeframe and wordage. As illustrated in table 3.1 below, one research aim can be broken into many enough research questions to complete a sound study.

Research questions, on the other hand, are a set of problems the proposed study intends to seek answers to. In a way, they are lines of enquiry the study plans to pursue and, hopefully, find answers to.

Because they are a breakdown of research aims, research questions are purposively narrower and more focused than research aims. Good research questions are also a useful tool for guiding the architecture of your proposed research, specifically the research design and execution. With regard to the literature review, it is good practice to report on and review what existing literature says on the same questions. In addition, research questions will also influence the methods choice and methodology decisions as everything you will do should be aimed at addressing the research questions. Consequently, we cannot emphasise the imperativeness of research questions enough.

*Table 3.1: Example of research aim and allied questions*

**Research aim**

The aim of this study is to investigate mental health problems among primary school children.

**Research questions**

To achieve this, the research will seek to answer the following research questions:

1) What is the prevalence of mental health problems among children in this primary school?
2) What is the range of mental health problems reported by these children?
3) How do these mental health problems impact on the children?
4) In what way do these children cope with these mental health problems?
5) What support are these children offered?
6) How effective do these children and their families find this support?

## 3.4.5 Significance of the research

The significance of the study section details the unique contribution the proposed study is expected to make to the existing literature or body of knowledge on the subject, topic or in the field. It is also an opportunity to explain an identified significant problem the study is hoped to solve. To be able to do this you may have identified, through your literature review, an area which is either receiving little attention or a topic under which the problems are well documented but there is very little discussion of solutions to these problems. Furthermore, it is essential to elucidate who will benefit from this study and in what way. Related to this, therefore, is presenting a compelling argument for why this research is timely – that is the extent to which the study addresses a current relevant issue in the field. This makes it important to explain in detail how exactly the proposed study will extend the current literature. To successfully write a significance of research argument, therefore, you need to be sufficiently familiar with the body of literature on your topic, especially consistent with the overall aim of the study.

### 3.4.6 Research methods and methodologies

The research methods and methodologies section of the research proposal indicates and justifies the means through which the proposed research project will be carried out, using which instruments and how. This tends to be influenced by the nature and design of study, research field precedent and, to a lesser extent, set timeframe for the study. Besides being the roadmap for the proposal, this section helps you demonstrate that you are aware of methods and methodologies consistent with your study in the context of the field within which your study falls. Again, owing to this being a research proposal, the methods and methodologies section is briefer than it is in the actual dissertation. Nonetheless, it is still an important part of the research proposal as it gives an indication as to the feasibility, potential validity, reliability and structural consistency of the intended study. Furthermore, if done well, this section will lay a good foundation for the eventual dissertation methods and methodologies chapter.

If wordage permits, it would also be a good idea to spell out who your intended sample is, indicative number of participants and justification thereof. Including this helps crystallise your ideas in the reader's eyes and, perhaps more importantly, strengthens your position in terms of your preparedness to carry out the research you are proposing.

### 3.4.7 Ethical issues

All research will likely present some ethical issues, and it is your responsibility to demonstrate that you are aware of them and have viable plans for addressing them before, during and after your study. As much as it is acceptable to read around general ethical issues surrounding research in your field of study, what is more important is showing your understanding, and consideration, of ethical issues specific to your own study, their likely effects if not tended to and what measures you have in place for minimising the impact of these issues on your study and your participants.

In general, ethical considerations in research surround the data collection process, the data output and its dissemination. The data collection process encompasses participant informed consent, the instruments to be utilised and how they will be deployed, the nature of questions or invasiveness of questions and their suitability for the target sample, how the data will be processed, stored or disposed of and how and where the research findings will be disseminated. At this stage, it is a brief section – though it still needs to be addressed.

The primary principle guiding the ethicality of your study is premised around doing no harm to the person and their dignity. In the broadest of senses, harm can be conceived as existing in two forms – physical and psychological. For instance, a study on children's mental health can have potential ethical issues to do with questions on what causes them distress triggering the experience of distress. In this case, as a researcher, you are expected to anticipate this before you get into the setting. What you then need to decide is what measure can be put in place to either minimise or avoid this potential harm from occurring as a consequence of your study. For example, it can be possible to observe children instead of interviewing them. To complement this, you may then go on to interview these children's teachers and/ or parents. Which decision you make should depend on your department's ethical guidance, which we strongly recommend you familiarise with and demonstrate you are aware of the same, and your discretion grounded in your personal, professional and academic experience. If in doubt, ask.

## 3.5 Summary

The research proposal has become one of social sciences degrees important assessment strategies. Considering the extent of its potential in preparing students for the dissertation, a core double-credit module on most degree programmes, it is easy to appreciate its centrality to academic study. This is one of the core reasons why we thought it important to include this chapter in this book. If your degree programme precludes the research proposal from its summative assessment tasks, you can still utilise the content of this chapter to complete your research ethics form which most departments and institutions require their students to do prior to embarking on a dissertation project.

At this point of the book, you should, therefore, be confident in your awareness and understanding of the meaning and purpose of a research proposal, its structure and content and how these should be approached in satisfactory preparation for your dissertation project. We now move on to the main dissertation project, starting with the literature review.

# 4 REVIEWING THE LITERATURE

## 4.1 Overview

Now that you have chosen your research topic, the next stage is to conduct your literature review in order to determine the significance of your research. The literature review provides background information to your research in order to help your reader understand and appreciate what your study entails and its significance. It also situates your research within the existing literature in your area of study whilst illustrating how your research contributes to the ongoing dialogue in your field of study. Most of your literature review will be written in your own words whilst also incorporating relevant ideas from the literature by paraphrasing them or quoting directly. When you quote, however, it is also imperative that you make a brief commentary on the quote, discussing why it is relevant to your research. A brief commentary also shows you are able to make sense of what you read, and you are able to adapt the ideas to your own study. When you paraphrase or quote from the original source, you will need to acknowledge your sources appropriately. Indicate with quotation marks where you quote directly from a source. That way, you avoid giving the reader an impression that the ideas you are presenting are your own. This chapter takes you through the steps that are involved in conducting a literature review as part of your dissertation. It also provides an example of how an introductory section to the literature review chapter can be approached.

## 4.2 What is a Literature Review?

A literature review explores and discusses relevant published material on your dissertation topic and research questions. Your literature review states the case for your study. Bolderston (2008: 86) states that a literature review is '… an informative, critical, and useful synthesis of a particular topic … what is known (and unknown) in the subject area, identify areas of controversy or debate, and help formulate questions that need further research …'. Thus, a literature review helps you situate your research within the existing body of literature whilst demonstrating your contribution to the ongoing dialogue on the subject within the wider academic community in your field of study.

## 4.3 The significance of a literature review

A literature review is an important element of your dissertation. It helps provide an academic justification for your study and how the readings have contributed to your understanding of the subject. According to Hart (1998), a literature review provides an understanding of the subject including:

- What has already been done on the topic.
- How the topic has been researched.
- What the key issues in the field are.
- Key theories/ models in the area of study.
- How these theories have been applied.
- Main criticisms made on existing body of work.

## 4.4 Key considerations

Before setting out on your literature search and literature survey journey, it is worth noting that not all literature is good literature and, in equal measure, not all sources are good sources. This is why you need to make deliberate decisions on what and where to search. Good literature decisions will make a positive contribution to the quality of your dissertation. The literature not only influences your literature review. Rather, it also impacts on the following:

- Your instrument design, if you need to design your own instruments.

- Choice of instruments, if you opt to use instruments that are already there, sometimes with slight modifications.
- Data collection methods and methodologies.
- Data analysis methods and methodologies.
- Data analysis and Interpretation.

Therefore, the literature search and literature survey decision should be taken seriously as the quality of your work is as good as the quality and sources of your literature.

## 4.5 Searching for and surveying new literature

The effectiveness of a literature search and literature survey depends on, to a great extent, the identification and use of appropriate search terms and an awareness of academically credible sources and platforms. It is also worth knowing where literature for your chosen topic is usually published and who the key authors are. Furthermore, trying different variations of your search terms will help explore available literature from multiple angles.

It is also a good idea to use multiple platforms and academically credible sources in order to cover a range of sources available for your research topic or subject. Your university library catalogue will likely yield some useful material. However, do not limit your search and survey to your library catalogue only since library catalogues tend to return search results based on what is available in that particular library, which is often limited. Over the years, Google Scholar has gained a reputation as a good source of academic material. Similar to Google Scholar is Microsoft's Microsoft Academic, which works in a similar way but may have slight differences in search returns. Beneath the search engines, you may find that some material requires payment while other material is open access. For material which requires payment, it is worth trying to use your institution login – in case the institution is already subscribed. Besides Google Scholar and Microsoft Academic, the British Library EThOS is another good source of academically credible literature with almost half a million doctoral theses on a wide range of topics including the one you are working on. You should not be put off using this library just because it stores doctoral theses. It is worth your while to have a look. Some of our past students have put doctoral theses to good use in their own dissertations.

It is to be expected that as soon as you start searching and surveying the literature on your topic, you will find yourself overwhelmed with the volume of source material. If you do not keep track of what you are doing, you will likely not remember whether you are repeating the same searches on the same platform and repeat-downloading some of the resources. Furthermore, you could end up carrying out excessive searches beyond the scope of your study. In light of this, we recommend that you determine the scope of your search so you are clear on what is relevant, what is important and what is not. To achieve this, it would be a good idea to use your research questions as a guide on what to look for in the literature and how. Our informed guess is that there will be something published on the research questions your study seeks answers to.

As we have indicated, it is important to keep track of your literature search and survey. In a simple – perhaps tabular – form, keep a record of the search terms you used, platforms consulted and a summary of returns. This is not an expectation for the successful completion of your dissertation. However, it is useful insofar as it helps you organise yourself and is a purposeful aid for systematic working. In the recent past, we have suggested to our students that including this literature search and survey record in the appendices of their dissertation does no harm to their work. If anything, it strengthens the work's authenticity argument.

## 4.6 Identify key relevant themes

Find a few relevant and key sources on the subject you are researching. It might be a good idea to go through these sources to see the range of sources that they referred to. This may be  particularly useful if you find a source that has reviewed literature in your field. This then helps you develop a substantial reference list for your work. Start by reviewing journal articles, books, policy documents, newspapers. Then evaluate the quality and relevance of what you read in relation to your research questions and focus. This will help you focus your reading and write-up process. Taylor and Procter (2008: online) offer helpful questions that may help you think through your literature review reading and write-up:

- "What is the **specific thesis, problem, or research question** that my literature review helps to define?"

- What **type** of literature review am I conducting? Am I looking at issues of theory? Methodology? Policy? Quantitative research (e.g. on the effectiveness of a new procedure)? Qualitative research (e.g., studies of loneliness among migrant workers)?
- What is the **scope** of my literature review? What types of publications am I using (e.g., journals, books, government documents, popular media)? What discipline am I working in (e.g., nursing psychology, sociology, medicine)?
- How good was my **information seeking**? Has my search been wide enough to ensure I have found all the relevant material? Has it been narrow enough to exclude irrelevant material? Is the number of sources I have used appropriate for the length of my paper?
- Have I **critically analysed** the literature I used? Do I follow through a set of concepts and questions, comparing items to each other in the ways they deal with them? Instead of just listing and summarizing items, do I assess them, discussing strengths and weaknesses?
- Have I cited and discussed studies **contrary** to my perspective?"

## 4.7 Structuring your literature review

We encourage you to carefully consider the structure of your literature review. Begin by reading relevant sources and outlining key themes that relate to your research questions. You will then need to organise these themes under subheadings by grouping together ideas that may be related. Start with the most general ideas, and progress to more specific discussions within each main heading. Wellington et al (2005:87) provide a useful guidance on how to approach your literature review write-up:

- "It should be framed by your research questions.
- It must relate to your study.
- It must be clear to the reader where it is going: keep signposting along the way.
- Wherever possible, use original source material rather than summaries or reviews by others.

37

- Be in control, not totally deferent to or 'tossed about by' previous literature.
- Be selective. Ask 'why am I including this?'
- It is probably best to treat it as a research project in its own right.
- Engage in a dialogue with the literature, you are not just providing a summary."

## 4.7.1 Literature review introduction: An Example

Your literature review chapter will begin with an introduction. It is important to include a brief outline of key ideas you are going to cover in your chapter. The example below is just an illustration of one way in which you could approach the introductory section of your literature review chapter. It is intended to help ensure you include key literature review elements. We advise you to follow the guidance you are provided by your supervisor:

1. The aim of this chapter is_____[state the aim of the chapter]. The chapter begins with a brief discussion of_____[key theoretical ideas you will draw on in order to make sense of the study. These are theories that will enable your readers to understand the subject and how you are approaching it].

2. Next, the chapter examines current perspectives that have contributed to ways in which _____ [state the problem you are researching] is constructed in _____[the context of your study]. Consideration is also given to _____

3. The chapter also explores and discusses relevant published literature relating to _____[state your focus] mapping developments on _____ [your key research questions that help narrow down your focus].

4. The chapter contends that_____[explain the key argument you are making in your study].

5. The conclusion _____ [explain how your conclusion is framed] whilst drawing on ____[ from _____(name the theory again ) perspective.

*(Adapted from Pat Thomson's 'sentence skeleton')*

## 4.7.2 The literature review body

In the body of the literature review is where you demonstrate your depth and breadth of knowledge and understanding on and of the subject. Drawing on Gabi (2015), the literature review body – also in light of your research questions – should achieve the following, ideally in this order:

1. Provide some key background to the topic or subject of study.
2. Identify and critically analyse dominant conceptual frameworks in the area of study.
3. Examine how the literature has answered the same or similar research questions as the ones you wish to carry out your investigation on.
4. Identify and explain gaps, limitations or weaknesses in how these questions have been addressed.
5. Explain how your research will seek to address some (not all) of these gaps, limitations or weaknesses.
6. Justify why your study will particularly seek to address the identified gaps, limitations or weaknesses and not the others.

Table 4.1 below expands on this process.

*Table 4.1: Writing the body of your literature review*

**1. Provide some key background to the topic or subject of study**
- Regarding the topic, what is the story so far?
- How did the topic begin to gain attention and why?
- What are the key turning points or milestones in the study of the topic or in the development of the phenomenon?
- How are people currently affected, positively or negatively, by the phenomenon to be studied?
- How prevalent is the phenomenon on the population from which you have drawn your sample?

**2. Identify and critically analyse dominant conceptual frameworks in the area of study**
- Theoretically, how is the phenomenon conceived?
- Here the purpose is to attempt to give the phenomenon being studied some academic meaning.

- You may want to consider any of the following: Models of the phenomenon; theories of the phenomenon, theoretical frameworks of the phenomenon. The expectation here is that you will critically examine these frameworks.
- Identify and justify which framework, out of these, your study will adopt. E.g. "This study will adopt … framework for the following reasons ….

**3. Examine how the literature has answered the same or similar research questions as the ones you wish to carry out your investigation on**

- It is important to align your literature review to your research questions. This will allow for consistency and compatibility with your data analysis.
- This also gives you ideas on how you may approach your own study in keeping with your research questions.

**4. Identify and explain gaps, limitations or weaknesses in how these questions have been addressed**

- What is it that the literature does not sufficiently address or answer?
- What is it that the literature does not pay enough attention to?

**5. Explain how your research will seek to address some (not all) of these gaps, limitations or weaknesses**

- In light of 4 above, how will your research address selected gaps, limitations or weaknesses?

**6. Justify why your study will particularly seek to address the identified gaps, limitations or weaknesses and not the others**

- Reasons for addressing selected gaps, limitations or weaknesses could be academic, professional or personal.
- e.g. "Addressing this limitation in the literature will, hopefully extend on what is known on … and, in the process, help address … in the workplace, which is still presenting major challenges."

### 4.7.3 The literature review conclusion

A good conclusion enhances the quality and strengthens the argument that has been put forward. Thus, the purpose of a conclusion – any conclusion – can be encapsulated into four functions: restate, highlight, recommend and predict (RHRP). Obviously, different authors will have different approaches to writing a conclusion, so you do not have to limit yourself to our model. Table 4.2 below expands on the RHRP conclusion model.

*Table 4.2: The RHRP conclusion model*

---

**1. Restate**
- Restate the aim/ purpose of the literature review
- e.g. "The aim(s) of this literature review was/ were ...

**2. Highlight**
- Highlight the key arguments made/ presented in the literature review.
- Highlight the concepts/ ideas/ points examined or explored.

**3. Recommend**
- In light of what you have highlighted in 2 above, what do you recommend deserves further research?
- Here you have an opportunity to present a case for arguing, in closing, why – therefore – your chosen focus is worth investigating.

**4. Predict**
- What developments in the literature or research do you anticipate to occur in light of what you examined in your literature review?
- e.g. "Consistent with observations made in this literature review, it seems ... will continue to attract attention from researchers and professionals, which is why it is important for this study to contribute to the discourse by seeking to address ...

---

## 4.8 Summary

This chapter has discussed the purpose of a literature review for your dissertation and how it helps set the scene and situate your research within existing literature in the field. It then explored a range of academically credible sites to get you started with the literature search and review processes. The chapter has made a case for the importance of utilising your research questions to structure your literature review chapter as this helps establish the context of your study's contribution to knowledge whilst further broadening your reader's understanding of the subject you are focusing on. We also noted that you will need to revisit your literature review when you analyse your data. Thus, it is important to ensure that there is constituency between and across your chapters in relation to the key argument you are making. You may want to consider your literature review as work-in-progress as you may realise that there is need to add more literature when you 'start explaining a point in writing that you find where your argument is weak, and you need to collect more evidence' ( The University of Manchester, 2018: Online). This chapter has also provided an example of phrases that are helpful to put across your arguments in a coherent and convincing way. It has further provided an example literature review introduction that served the purpose of illustrating an effective way of writing an introduction that captures the essence of a literature review chapter. Guidance on the literature review body and conclusion has also been provide. In the following chapter, focus shifts to data collection methods and methodologies.

# 5 DATA COLLECTION METHODS AND METHODOLOGIES

## 5.1 Overview

Data collection, as a fundamental part of a dissertation research project, should also be approached with careful consideration. This is when the evidence for what you are investigating is gathered and answers to your research questions sought. As such, what you do, the instruments you use to carry this out and how you undertake the process using the selected instruments is of much importance. The focus of this chapter is some of the most common data collection methods among students and guidance on how these may be put to best use in keeping with research convention. Consistent with this, the chapter also takes particular interest in research instrumentation – that is instrument design and deployment.

The structure of this chapter is in three main parts. The first part explores key research methods and methodologies. The next part deals with instrument design and deployment decisions and procedure. Finally, a summary of the key points of this chapter is presented.

## 5.2 What are methods and what are methodologies?

Earlier, we noted the difference between methods and methodologies. Methods refers to the *what* while methodology is the *how*. The research method is the data collection *technique* used. The research methodology is the *process*, that is how the research technique is implemented or put to use. In a dissertation project both methods and methodologies are important. Essentially, there must be consistency between methods and methodologies, and the two must suit the research topic and context.

The most common research methods employed at degree level are categorised into three main types, that is qualitative, quantitative and mixed-methods. We consider each of these in turn next.

## 5.3 Qualitative research methods

In a rather general sense, qualitative research methods are non-numerical, subjective means of studying phenomena in their contexts (Silverman, 2017). These methods include observations, interviews, text and pictorial and audio analyses. Some of the most popular qualitative research methods among students are diaries, interviews, focus groups and observations. The more adventurous ones have incorporated images and artefacts into their studies.

### 5.3.1 Diaries

For degree research purposes, participant diaries tend to be non-invasive in nature. These can either be designed specifically for the research or just general diaries or plain notebooks completed in a more flexible way. Study-specific diaries are purposive, structured and guide participants on sequence and content of what is to be recorded. In this case, the diaries can be formatted as a series of forms (Robson and McCartan, 2016). Non study-specific diaries tend to be thoughts documented as they occur, regardless of relevance to the research. In this case, relevance and significance of diary entries to the study is then determined at the data analysis stage.

*Table 5.1: Structured and unstructured diaries*

| Structured diaries | Unstructured diaries |
| --- | --- |
| Study-specific | Non study-specific |
| Research questions based | Not always based on RQs |
| Designed by researcher | No particular design |
| Narrow focus | Broad, general focus |
| Predetermined themes | No particular theme |

*Table 5.2: Example of a structured diary*

| |
|---|
| Date: 30/09/2018<br>Location: Classroom<br><br>1.   Summary of what happened<br>..............................................................................<br>..............................................................................<br>..............................................................................<br><br>2.   Stressors<br>..............................................................................<br>..............................................................................<br>..............................................................................<br><br>3.   Coping strategies<br>..............................................................................<br>..............................................................................<br>..............................................................................<br><br>4.   Effectiveness of coping strategies<br>..............................................................................<br>..............................................................................<br>.............................................................................. |

*Table 5.3: Example of an unstructured diary*

| |
|---|
| 30 September 2018<br>Record of events<br><br>AM<br>..............................................................................<br>..............................................................................<br>..............................................................................<br><br>PM<br>..............................................................................<br>..............................................................................<br>.............................................................................. |

There are a number of considerations to take into account when you process, analyse and report on respondents' diary entries. As there is likelihood of some individual or third-party personal information to be included in the diaries, care must be taken in the handling of this data. At the minimum, all participant identities must be anonymised. One way of doing this using pseudonyms. If excerpts of the data will be included in the appendices it is recommended that people's and, in most cases, settings' identities are blacked out. Work in conjunction with your supervisor to be clear on your department's or institution's policy on data protection as this may be different across different institutions, departments and programmes.

## 5.3.2 Interviews

Interviews remain a popular research method for most social sciences students owing to its perceived accessibility. The methodology primarily involves the researcher asking a participant or participants a series of questions linked to set research aims. Although some researchers use technology such as phone calls or video calls, most research interviews are still carried out in person. Depending on the researcher's aims and research design, interviews can either be **structured, semi-structured** or **unstructured**.

**Structured interviews**, also referred to as standardised interviews, have predetermined questions and sequence in which these questions are asked. Hence, the researcher asks all interviewees the same questions in a consistent manner. This type of interviews enables the researcher to make comparisons between respondents as part of the data analysis process. Where more than one researcher conducts the same study, potential for consistency across interviewers is much higher than in the other two interview types. Moreover, the interviewer will find this interview type helpful in sticking to the aims of the research. A major problem with this type of interview is that it overlooks contextual and individual respondent differences which may call for adapting questions to context, individuals and responses being given. Follow-up questions are not asked even when they might be of assistance in shedding more light on what an individual respondent may have said.

In **semi-structured interviews** the researcher has a predetermined list of questions they intend to ask the interviewee. In most cases, the interview process will generally follow a predetermined sequence, although opportunities to ask follow-up questions, for clarification or just to probe further, may be made use of. On the whole, however, interviewee responses are closely influenced by the researcher's questions and sequencing. The key advantage of semi-structured interviews is that they help the researcher and the interviewee to stick as close to the research aims as possible, thereby saving time, relative to unstructured interviews. A major criticism of this form of interviews, nonetheless, is that they sometimes constrain respondents on how they answer questions as flexibility is still limited.

**Unstructured interviews**, conversely, offer respondents more flexibility in how they answer questions posed by researchers and how they frame these answers (Edwards and Holland, 2013). Thus, to get the interview started, the researcher will ask just one very broad question – which will, of course, be linked to the research aim(s) – and let the participant respond in their own way, with minimum to no interruption. The role of the researcher in this context, then, is to follow themes emerging from the interviewee's responses and trying to understand meanings embedded within the interviewee's responses. One of the arguments for adopting this interview form, therefore, that respondents will likely say more when what they say is not stifled by a pre-set form and sequence. They feel freer and in control which will likely generate more data for the researcher. A major shortcoming of this form of interview, though, is that it may use up more time to address a research aim. It is also possible that data excess to requirements of the research aims will be generated.

*Table 5.4: When interviews are most appropriate*

- To find out individuals' perceptions on a subject or topic
- To explore individuals' understandings of experiences or events
- To gather individual historical accounts
- To obtain an in-depth insight into a phenomenon
- To follow up on emerging results from a preceding survey

## Effective interviews

To make the most of interviews it is key that you know beforehand what exactly you want out of the interview. To this end, planning and careful thought are important. By the time you get at the stage where you are preparing to conduct interviews as part of your data collection you should have satisfied yourself that the interview is the most appropriate data collection method for your study. So, you must already have set research aims and research questions. Thus, the next consideration you should make is what it is that you should do to conduct an effective interview, one which will generate the best possible data for your research aims and research questions. Table 5.5 below gives you some of the key effectiveness considerations to be made before you undertake interviews for research purposes.

*Table 5.5: Key considerations for an effective interview*

| |
|---|
| 1. Are the interview questions relevant to the study? |
| 2. Do the questions address the research aims and research questions? |
| 3. Are the questions appropriate for the interviewee? |
| 4. Are the questions easy to understand for the type of interviewee? |
| 5. Is the interview of an appropriate length? |
| 6. Is the sequence of interview questions logical? |

Alongside these considerations, you should also be aware of common pitfalls to avoid, the most common of which are listed below.

*Table 5.6: What to avoid in an interview*

| |
|---|
| 1. Lengthy questions. |
| 2. Double-barrelled questions. |
| 3. Leading questions. |
| 4. Bias. |
| 5. Presumptuousness. |

During the interview you should always bear in mind that you are interviewing *to find out*, not to show off what you know or to impress the interviewee. Therefore, stay calm and consistently respectful. Below is an outline of interview etiquette that will help you conduct an appropriate interview.

*Table 5.7: Research interview etiquette*

| |
|---|
| 1. Listen more than you talk. |
| 2. Keep the tone of your voice appropriate. |
| 3. Do not be argumentative. |
| 4. If you need to probe or follow up, do so appropriately |
| 5. Speak audibly. |
| 6. Interview in good faith. |
| 7. Assume all answers are given in good faith, even those you personally do not agree with. |

There is no universally accepted 'right' way to conduct an interview. However, some approaches are more effective than others. That said, most of what you do, and how you do it, is mostly at your discretion as you are in the interview context with your interviewees. With this in mind, the interview sequence below (table 5.8) is given as guide only, based on most commonly followed approaches in social sciences in accordance with Robson (2002).

*Table 5.8: Most common interview sequence*

**1. Interview introduction**
- Thank the interviewee for agreeing to take part in the interview.
- State the aim of the interview.
- Also indicate that it is part of your study on a specific topic.
- Give an indication of approximately how long it will be.

**2. Warm-up question**
- Start with an easy, general question to ease the participant into the interview.
- Most researchers start with: "Briefly tell me about your career so far."
- This will provide important background data to the interview.

**3. Main interview body**
- After the warm-up question, interviewees are usually ready for the main body.

#### 4. 'Wind-down' questions
- These are easy questions intended to gently end the interview.
- There may be other things the interviewee wishes to say which may not have been covered in the interview body.
- Usually, researchers ask questions like: "Are there any school readiness tips you would offer new teachers?"
- Another good wind-down question would be: "Is there anything else you wish to add?"

#### 5. Closure
- It is good interview etiquette to also thank the interviewee at the end.
- Depending on context, you could also tell the interviewee what will happen next with regard to your research or their access to the data, if you have any arrangements along these lines.

### 5.3.3 Focus groups

Focus groups, loosely described as group interviews, are more of group discussions than they are interviews. They are usually used when a researcher seeks to find out the collective, rather than the individual, understanding of or perspective on specific phenomena. The researcher will seek to draw insights on a group's collective thinking on a subject or topic. Unlike in interviews, where the process takes a straightforward question-and-answer format, the role of the researcher in a focus group scenario is to facilitate discussion (Robson and McCartan, 2016). Interest is in range, rather than depth, of discussion as there will likely be a plethora of topics emerging from the group discussion. It is possible that some focus group participants may change their position on a topic or subject as a result of others' contributions.

Ensure every participant is clear on what the purpose of the focus group is and what it is that they are expected to do or contribute. Issues to do with the duration and format of the focus group are some of the things most participants will need information about. Effective focus groups occur when everyone concerned knows the extent of their role and the exact purpose and duration of the undertaking. Therefore, communication is crucial to group dynamics within a focus group. Both verbal and non-verbal communication is critical to the dynamics of a focus group discussion. You should also be aware of the various body language signals from across the group. For a skilled facilitator, they will be able to tell if participants are unclear on what direction to take, need further assistance or are ready to move on to the next stage. You will also know when to intervene and when to step back, depending on the circumstances. At all times, endeavour to keep the focus group consistently appropriate and respectful.

Confidentiality is important and should be emphasised at the beginning of the focus group discussion. Parenthetically, it happens to be one of the biggest challenges of undertaking focus groups. This is mainly because this research method goes on in a group context where, almost inevitably, confidential information will be discussed. Controlling and ensuring the safe handling of this information will remain an issue. That is why care must be taken when identifying participants for focus group research. Mishandling personal data has damaging ramifications for the research, the researcher, the participants and the subjects of that data. Some of these consequences are ethical, but others could even be legal. So, exercise absolute caution.

There are further issues researchers need to be mindful of before they embark on a focus group endeavour. First is the challenge of ensuring a balance of participation between and among participants. This is especially so where some participants are more dominant than others. What must be avoided is a situation where the researcher will get away from the focus group with the views of just a handful of focus group members. As much as possible, it is best to gather a range of perspectives to enable you to have findings which are an accurate reflection of the composition of the focus group. That is one of the reasons why a core skill a focus group researcher must have, and should put to use, is the ability to moderate the process (Robson and McCartan, 2016). Should you adopt focus groups as a research method for your dissertation, you will need to include in the methodology chapter an explanation of how you addressed these issues in your study and why.

Nagle and Williams (2013) outline a five-stage process for conducting a focus-group as shown in table 5.9 below.

*Table 5.9: The focus group process*

| |
|---|
| **1. Define study purpose or aim** |
| • Study purpose helps direct your focus group. |
| • In light of the above, be clear what it is that you want to get out of the focus group. |
| **2. Define population and sample** |
| • What kind of participants are best for the research aims you have? |
| • How many participants do you need for this project? |
| • What is/ are the demographic(s), e.g. age group, gender, professional background etc? |
| **3. Facilitation** |
| • What format will the focus group take? |
| • What will the scope of discussion be, e.g. themes, topic etc? |
| • What level of participation is expected from individuals and from the group? |
| • How long will the focus group last? |
| **4. Analysis** |
| • Initial analysis can begin during the focus group as the researcher notes key points and observations. An argument can be made that active listening and observation involves some form of analysis. |
| • Main analysis should begin immediately after the focus group while the proceedings are still fresh in the mind of the researcher. |
| • Systematic analysis is better than arbitrary annotations. |
| **5. Reporting** |
| • The purpose of reporting influences its direction. |
| • Reporting in a dissertation means you will have to adhere to academic convention within your institution and department. |
| • Report ethically. |
| • Interpretations and analyses should be backed by, and consistent with, the data. |
| • Avoid misreporting, over-reporting or underreporting. |
| • Uphold confidentiality at all times. |
| • Remember the importance of context in the interpretation and analysis of the data. |

Focus group briefs take different forms, depending on their purpose. Below (table 5.10), we give a suggested template outline based on the World Health Organisation (2018: online) and the University of Arizona (2018: online) we think will be helpful for a systematic focus group study.

*Table 5.10: Focus group template*

**Focus group:** [Insert topic here]

**Consent**
- Briefly describe the research purpose.
- Briefly describe the approximate number of participants who will take part.
- Briefly explain what kind of topic or topics, hence questions, will be asked.
- Also say what these questions are hoped to achieve in the context of the research.
- Highlight that: "Your participation in this focus group is voluntary and you can withdraw at any time without giving reasons why at no expense or penalty to you."
- Highlight the importance of respecting other participants' privacy and confidentiality in connection to the focus group proceedings and content.
- It is important that you leave a space for participants to append their signature, printed name and date to indicate that they have read and fully understood the research information provided on the form and that they agree to participate.

**Focus group demographic details questionnaire**
- Age
- Sex
- Professional background
- Professional experience in years
- Note this is provided in writing. So, issue this as questionnaire handout. **Do not ask demographic questions orally as part of the focus group.**

- What, and whether, to include in this section depends on your research aim(s). However, generally, this helps provide background of your participants, and therefore contextualise their responses.

**Discussion outline**

**1. Facilitator's welcome, introduction and instructions to participants**
- Welcome and thank you.
- Introduction of focus group topic, focus and purpose.
- Anonymity and confidentiality reassurance to participants.
- Ground rules, e.g. one person speaking at a time, no set order of speaking, no right or wrong answer, no obligation to agree with others etc.
- Ask if anyone has questions before proceeding.

**2. Warm up**
- Introductions. Who is who?

**3. Introductory question**
- Ask for any volunteers who are happy to share their experience in general regarding the topic.

**4. Focus group body**
- Ask about participants' general attitudes towards, say, a given list of issues.
- Ask participants to discuss what they have done in their practice regarding these issues.
- Ask about other stakeholders' roles, e.g. government, employers etc, depending on your topic.
- e.g. What are your perspectives regarding the school readiness checklist provided?
- e.g. What do you think are the key influences on school readiness in your experience?

**5. Concluding question**
- Ask participants what they consider highlights of the focus group.
- You can ask them a reflective question at this point.
- e.g. In reflection, what would you consider are the key issues surrounding school readiness?

> - e.g. Is there anything you have changed your position on as a result of participating in this focus group? Why?
> - e.g. What, therefore, do you think is the way forward insofar as school readiness is concerned?
>
> ### 6. Conclusion of focus group
> - Thank the group for participating.
> - Reiterate how valuable their contribution will be to your research.
> - Point to the group how and where they can raise anything they are unhappy with in regard to the conduct of the focus group.
> - Reassure participants that their anonymity will be upheld in your study.

Focus group analyses are conducted in a similar manner to other qualitative data. However, take into consideration the data collection methodology and context as this will influence how the methodology or methodologies will be utilised. For a more detailed consideration of data analyses, please refer to chapter 8.

### 5.3.4 Observations

Observations count among the most popular research methods in social sciences. Consistent with this trend, most of the students we have had over the years have tended to favour this data collection technique, among others. One of the reasons our students have given for choosing this method is its flexibility, hence accessibility to researchers operating at different levels in different contexts for a plethora of purposes. At degree level, there are a variety of scenarios where observational methods are appropriate. We list the main ones in table 5.11 below.

*Table 5.11: When observation is an appropriate research method*

- For events or experiences that can be ethically accessed.
- Where the researcher wants to carry out in-depth multi-faceted investigation, i.e. the visual, the behaviour, the speech, the physical context.
- Small groups.
- Observed phenomena occurring over a short time.
- Observed phenomena are frequent, i.e. recurrent. These could be routines, a particular lesson on a particular day of the week etc.
- When the researcher has time to carry out a series of observations.
- When you want to find out behaviours and interactions of research participants in a specified context.

## Units of observation

One question most students ask is: What exactly do researchers observe when they get into the research setting? In a field as complex as social sciences, the answer to the question is as frustrating as it is disappointing to many students who are looking for exactness in guidance they get. The fulcrum of the matter is that observation, like most qualitative research methods, is an inexact endeavour. What we can say with certainty is that the research process must be rigorous and systematic enough to be academically defensible. For guidance purposes, Robson and McCartan (2016) get close to the pith of rigour expectations in their broad outline of a list of observation dimensions – please see table 5.12 below. These can also be referred to as units of observation and, subsequently at analysis stage, units of analysis.

*Table 5.12: Dimensions of observations*

**Space**
- Layout or organisation of space influences behaviour and interactions.
- What impact does space have on who and what you are observing?

**Actors**
- Names and relevant details of people involved.
- Roles of individuals in the context.
- Are these roles fixed?
- Are the roles predetermined or negotiated?
- What impact do these roles have on who and what is being observed?

**Activities**
- Collective activities of actors.
- What activities do individuals in the group carry out?
- How do these individual activities contribute to, or influence, the collective activities of the group?

**Objects/ Artefacts**
- Physical elements e.g. furniture, displays etc.
- This could be pictures of past activities, trips or mementos/ souvenirs.
- What do these objects or artefacts tell the observer about the values, culture and routines of the groups?
- Is there anything in these objects and artefacts that gives you access to the history, or moments in history, of the group?
- Could there be anything historical captured in the objects or artefacts that could possibly link to present behaviour?

**Acts**
- Specific, unstructured individual actions.
- List acts you consider significant as they occur.
- Sometimes what is significant may be difficult to determine at the time of occurrence, so record as much as you can.

**Events**

- These are particular occasions, e.g. meetings, seminars, CPD sessions etc.
- Dissimilar to acts, these tend to be structured and/ or organised.
- In a sense, most of what happens here is scripted.
- If allowed into events as a student researcher, this could be a window into the formal activities of the setting.
- Keep an eye on what is influencing these events and how they, in turn, influence acts.

**Time**

- Sequence of events.
- In what sequence do events in the setting occur?
- What could be influencing this sequence?
- What impact does this sequence have?

**Goals**

- What actors are attempting to accomplish.
- What do individuals in the setting wish to achieve by behaving the way they do?
- What are the key drivers of these goals?
- What do these goals tell you about the people pursuing them?
- What interaction is there between individual and group goals?
- In what way does this pursuit of goals influence group interactions?

**Feelings**

- Emotions in the particular context.
- What moods can you observe at a different times?
- What could be triggering these feelings?
- What are the individual feelings?
- What are the collective feelings?
- How do these influence the group dynamics?

## 5.3.5 Visual methodologies

Throughout history, images – alongside artefacts – have played a critical role in human life. Take, for example, how historians and archaeologists have consistently utilised visuals to extract significant information about different points in history and drawn some links to what is happening in the modern day. Consider cave art, mostly paintings and engravings left on cave walls, for example. They have provided invaluable access into historical societies' thoughts, cultures and hobbies even long after what is captured in them has passed.

In the present day, although we do not so much do cave paintings and engravings as done in the past, images and artefacts remain central to the modern society's way of life. The advent of the smartphone, arguably the most photographed era of all time, has ushered in heightened interest in image production and storage. The images taken are displayed in publicly accessible places like classroom and office walls, websites and in institutional publications such as periodicals. Similarly, artefacts such as souvenirs from trips, calendars and objects made in art classes are a common feature of setting articles.

In a way, images and artefacts – up to a point – immortalise moments-in-time, events, beliefs and ways of life. They tell a rich, powerful and often compelling story. Taken in their context, images and artefacts carry a lot of meaning and significance to place and people. Therefore, they are as important to a researcher's attempt to unpick phenomena and people as acts and events in situ.

Using visual materials like images and artefacts is, thus, gaining respectability traction as a genuine qualitative data collection methodology. While it is possible to carry out a completely visual materials-based study – which is complex and, therefore, requires advanced research skills, most students use visual materials as part of a mixed-methods design where the visual material data complements other data forms. Either way, to optimise the role of visual materials in a research project, there is need for a systematic, rigorous approach in the collection and analysis of image and artefact data. First, it is appropriate to consider when it is key to incorporate visual methodologies in a research design.

*Table 5.13: When it is appropriate to utilise visual methodologies*

- When the images and/ or objects are accessible.
- These images and/ or objects are an integral part of the group's or individuals in the study context.
- When use of these images helps address the research aims(s) and/ or answer the research questions.
- When these images and/ or artefacts complement other data collected in the setting.
- When the researcher wants to find out participants' interpretation of the images and/ or objects.
- When observations cannot be made directly.

In most research contexts, images and/ or artefacts represent – and often capture – peoples' and societies' treasured memories. They speak to who these people are or aspire to be. Some of them could conjure a traumatic present or past. It is unsurprising that some of these images and/ or artefacts have a sacred place in their subjects' lives. And yet, still, some images and artefacts may be a source of pride for the research participants. Therefore, images and artefacts should be approached sensitively. Below we outline some ethical considerations for conducting research using visual methodologies, a valuable, yet sensitive, approach.

*Table 5.14: Ethical considerations for visual methodologies*

**1. Pre-existing or concurrently generated**
- Visuals for this methodology either pre-exist or will be concurrently generated with your research.
- Combining pre-existing and research-generated material can augment claims of rigour.

**2. What the images and artefacts represent**
- Are they private?
- Are they individual or group images and/ or artefacts?
- What emotion do these images and/ or artefacts invoke?

**2. Situational interpretation of the images and artefacts**
- What is considered an acceptable interpretation of these images and/ artefacts?
- Are they controversial?

### 3. Religio-political significance

- Some images and artefacts have caused consternation among certain communities. So, take care how and what you use.
- Do the images and/ or artefacts carry a strong religious or political significance to the participants or their community?

### 4. Usability in research

- Can the images and artefacts be utilised in a scholarly context?
- Are there limiting clauses attached to the use of, and reporting on, these images and artefacts? Some settings may only allow you to comment on the existence of the images and artefacts, as opposed to using the actual images and artefacts in your dissertation. Find out first.

### 5. Informed consent

- Has informed consent to use these images and artefacts been granted?
- When negotiating access into the setting, you need to provide sufficient information to the setting and/ or participants on your intention to use the settings' images and artefacts.

Planned use of artefacts and images in research is more systematic and rigorous than incidental utilisation. Right at the beginning of your research process, during the research design stage, you need to purposively consider if you will utilise artefacts and images. Once this is done, you must plan for this aspect of your research. Here are the primary planning contemplations you need to take into account.

*Table 5.15: Visual methodologies planning*

| |
|---|
| **1. What type of images and artefacts?**<br>▪ Pictures?<br>▪ Artefacts or objects?<br>▪ Videos?<br><br>**2. Selection criteria**<br>▪ How will the images and artefacts be selected?<br>▪ Which images and artefacts?<br>▪ Extent of sensitivity in usage.<br>▪ Relevance to the research focus.<br><br>**3. How these images and artefacts will be used**<br>▪ Will you publish the images and artefacts in the report, or will you just make reference to them? Clarify this with the setting.<br><br>**4. How these images and artefacts will be analysed**<br>▪ Which analysis methodolog(y/ies) will be used to make sense of the images and artefacts?<br>▪ Do the chosen analysis methodologies suit the images and artefacts?<br><br>**5. Visual methodologies research tradition**<br>▪ Are your intended processes, from data collection to data analysis, consistent with visual methodologies research tradition?<br>▪ Are the processes sufficiently rigorous for degree level of study? Here, it is a good idea to consider your dissertation learning outcomes. |

## 5.4 Quantitative research methods

Quantitative research methods are numerical and, therefore, are concerned with objective measurements utilising "...statistical, mathematical, or numerical analysis of data collected through polls, questionnaires, and surveys..." (University of Southern California, 2018: online). It is important , however, to note that the notion of objectivity is not that straightforward as the administration and interpretation of these measurements is, at best, contestable. Take questionnaires, for example; these are self-completed by participants. Even though they complete the same questionnaire, what one measure means to one respondent is likely to be different to what it means to the next. The same observation can be made at data analysis where the interpretation of the same dataset usually varies across different researchers. Such caveats should be taken into account when it comes to discussing validity and reliability in the dissertation.

Examples of quantitative data collection methods are opinion polls, referenda, censuses, rating scales and questionnaire surveys. These methods are very similar in their design and application as there tends to be an overlap in their content type and formatting. The major difference is in their use rather than their formatting, which can sometimes be alike.

**Opinion polls** are predominantly used to solicit a target group's views on a subject, institution or to capture a group's collective feeling on an issue. An example is an effort to find out favourability of a political leader on issues like the group's confidence in the leader's leadership or how they feel about the economy.

**Referenda**, on the other hand, are useful for collective decision making. Normally, these tend to be binary yes/no questions. Good examples are the Brexit and the Scottish independence referenda.

**Censuses** are utilised in the counting of subjects or populations. These can range from simple counts of the size of populations or number of households to more specific demographic aspects such as age, sex or ethnicity. Censuses will be deployed either by paper or electronically, usually by official institutions.

**Rating scales** are, by their very nature, evaluative. For example, you may want to find out respondents' assessment of different dimensions of the quality of service they are getting such as value for money, excellence of customer care and effectiveness of communication.

**Questionnaire surveys**, unlike the other quantitative methods identified above, are more general – that is they do not have a particular feature distinguishing them from the rest of these methods. In research practice, questionnaires can, therefore, be a combination of all these methods and more. The primary object of questionnaire surveys is collecting data on a range of dimensions in the same instance. Predictably, the main instrument utilised in this data gathering method is the questionnaire. Questionnaire surveys generally utilise either paper or electronic questionnaires. Electronic questionnaires largely eliminate the data entry stage as the dataset is generated as respondents submit their completed questionnaires. This significantly reduces data input errors. Questionnaires can be structured, unstructured or semi-structured. Structured questionnaires have closed questions with pre-set sets of responses from which the respondent selects one or any number of options as directed in the questionnaire instructions. The options given are standardised from what the researcher anticipates to be the likely responses to the questions. On the same breadth, the respondent is being limited to just those responses given as options. Unstructured questionnaires, on the other hand, are open-ended. In this context, this means that questions in this type of questionnaire do not come with predefined answers. Therefore, participants are free to answer the questions as they wish, in their own words. Semi-structured questionnaires, in contrast, are a combination of structured and unstructured questions. Hence, both closed and open-ended questions will be included in this type of questionnaire.

Due to the questionnaire's capacity to combine all other identified quantitative data collection methods, in figure 5.1 below we give a semi-structured questionnaire example with a variety of questions to give you a range of ideas on how you may design your own.

*Figure 5.1: Semi-structured questionnaire example*

## Teachers' perspectives on school readiness questionnaire

Thank you for taking your time to complete this anonymous questionnaire as part of a study on primary school teachers' perspectives on school readiness.

### Section 1: About you
Sex: Male ☐  Female ☐
Teaching experience: ☐ years

### Section 2: Families' role
On a scale of 1 (strongly disagree) to 5 (strongly agree), please indicate to what extent you agree with the following statements.

|  | 1 | 2 | 3 | 4 | 5 |
|---|---|---|---|---|---|
| Parents are a key influence on children's school readiness |  |  |  |  |  |
| Parents are to blame for poor school readiness |  |  |  |  |  |
| Family poverty leads to poor school readiness |  |  |  |  |  |
| Parents' education level influences school readiness |  |  |  |  |  |

### Section 3: Factors affecting school readiness
Please rank the extent of importance each of the following factors has to school readiness. Use the scale of 1 (not important at all) to 5 (very important).

|  | 1 | 2 | 3 | 4 | 5 |
|---|---|---|---|---|---|
| Child's age |  |  |  |  |  |
| Child's diet |  |  |  |  |  |
| Family affluence |  |  |  |  |  |
| Type of neighbourhood |  |  |  |  |  |
| Child's physical health |  |  |  |  |  |
| Child's stage of development |  |  |  |  |  |
| Child's emotional wellbeing |  |  |  |  |  |

### Section 4: Your competency
With regard to children who come into your setting at a low level of school readiness, please indicate with an 'X' in the scale below how confident you are in your ability to sufficiently support these children (0 being no confidence at all and 10 being very high confidence).

```
|   |   |   |   |   |   |   |   |   |   |   |
0   1   2   3   4   5   6   7   8   9   10
```

**Section 5: Supporting children and families**

It has been widely recommended that schools support families in making children school-ready. Please rank the following recommendations in order of importance by appending an appropriate rank position against each recommendation. 1 is most important and 5 is least important.

- Hold consultation meetings with families to establish children's needs before they join the school.
- Start school-run school readiness clubs for parents and children.
- Obtain children's developmental progress reports from their carers prior to them joining the school.
- Enlist services of educational psychologists.
- Identify children at risk of not being school ready.

**Section 6: Improving school readiness practice**

Please briefly outline in the space below your suggestions for improving practice in supporting children who come into your setting insufficiently school-ready.

................................................................................
................................................................................
................................................................................
................................................................................
........................

When designing a questionnaire, there is need to ensure the data it will generate will be sound. To achieve this, your questionnaire must meet basic validity and reliability canons. With regard to this, table 5.16 below (adapted from Robson, 2002)) outlines the basic criteria your questionnaire must satisfy.

*Table 5.16: Key questionnaire design points to note*

## 1. Use simple language

- Using simple language enables respondents to understand the questionnaire.
- The soundness of responses depends on participants' understanding of the questions and instructions.

## 2. Give clear instructions

- Respondents should be clear what it is they are being asked to do.
- Know the kind of language your intended participants comprehend.

## 3. Keep questions as short as possible

- Short questions increase understanding.
- Short questions help in keeping time spent to complete the questionnaire at the minimum.
- Long questions may discourage potential participants from completing the questionnaire as people are usually busy.

## 4. Avoid double-barrelled questions

- e.g. "Please indicate the impact age and/ or poverty has on school readiness on a scale of 1 (very low impact) to 5 (very high impact). A response to this question will be difficult to interpret. For example, is the score given to do with the impact of age, poverty or both? You cannot say, with certainty, which factor the score relates to. Rather, split the question into two – one on the impact of age and the other on the impact of poverty.

## 5. Avoid questions in the negative

- e.g. "From statements below, please tick the ones you do not agree with." The likelihood is that respondents will proceed to tick statements they agree with, despite the instruction – mostly out of habit and human nature. People are generally used to being asked to select what they agree with and are, therefore, drawn to what they agree with.

**6. Questions must only cover subjects or topics respondents have knowledge on**

- This increases the validity and reliability of your findings.
- There is no point asking participants questions they are not knowledgeable on.
- This goes back to identifying the appropriate sample for your study.

**7. Questions must mean the same thing to all respondents**

- Consistency in the understanding of questions enhances the validity of your questionnaire.
- Consistency in meaning helps your questionnaire measure what it purports to measure
- Analysis of findings will be difficult if questions mean different things to different respondents.

**8. Avoid ambiguous questions**

- Ambiguous questions are those which have more than one meaning. This makes them vague to respondents.
- Interpretation, hence analysis, of responses to ambiguous questions is difficult.

**9. Avoid direct questions on sensitive topics**

- Generally, people are uncomfortable answering direct questions on sensitive subjects, even anonymously.
- e.g. "To what extent has bereavement impacted on your ability to support children you teach, on a scale of 1 (no impact at all) to 5 (much impact)?" This will likely evoke negative memories and emotions in respondents, which may lead to them not completing the questionnaire. Instead, rephrase to: "To what extent does bereavement impact on teachers' ability to support children they teach, on a scale of 1 (no impact at all) to 5 (much impact)?"

**10. Use personal wording if you want respondents to comment on their feelings**

- This must be considered in the context of 9 above. This is best if the question is not sensitive.

- If the topic is not sensitive, use personal words like *you* and *your*.
- e.g. "Please indicate the extent to which *you* agree with the following statement on a scale of 1 (strongly disagree) to 5 (strongly agree)".

## 5.5 Mixed-methods research

In recent years, adoption of mixed-methods research design has been gradually gaining momentum. One of the reasons for the growth in popularity has been that mixed-methods research combines the two research traditions – qualitative and quantitative methods (Creswell and Plano-Clark, 2007). This applies to both data collection and data analysis. The main rationale for combining quantitative and qualitative research methods is complementarity, that is combining strengths of the two whereby weaknesses in one method are offset by strengths in the other. Depending on your mixed-methods research design, data collection can be done either concurrently or separately.

Similar to other research methods, the use of the mixed-methods approach is based on a number factors. The main ones are the research topic, focus, aims and scope. There is also need to consider other practical issues like extent of access to the research setting and time available to conduct the study. Note that, as with any other research design you may adopt, you will need to justify the adoption of the mixed-methods approach in your research.

Another important point is the sequencing of the data collection process and proportionality of significance of each constituent research method to the whole research design. In some cases, one research method will play a central role while the other one is auxiliary. In other cases, research methods have equal importance to the overall project. Either way, the constituent method significance proportion should be reflected in the analysis for consistency. If used appropriately, a mixed-methods research design strengthens the validity and reliability integrity of the study. Below is an outline of the most common arguments in favour of employing the mixed-methods approach identified by the Grand Canyon University (2018).

*Tables 5.17: Common reasons for adopting the mixed-methods approach*

| |
|---|
| **1. Methodology triangulation** |
| ■ Comparing results to establish if results from the different methodologies used validate, corroborate or converge with each other. |
| **2. Complementarity** |
| ■ Offsetting weaknesses of, or enhancing results from one method with results from, another used within the same study. |
| **3. Development** |
| ■ Building on an idea emerging from results of one method with results from a complementing method. |
| **4. Initiation** |
| ■ Using different methods within a study to look for contradictions and new perspectives. |
| **5. Expansion** |
| ■ To extend existing knowledge on the topic or subject. |

## 5.6 Research paradigms: What they are and their place

The term *paradigm* is defined variously in research literature. In the context of research, Kuhn (1962) is credited for having first used the term to mean "a philosophical way of thinking" (Kivunja and Kuyini, 2017:26). It can be described as knowledge influences underpinning one's perspectives and interpretations of phenomena. The argument here is that the main reason why different people understand and interpret phenomena, and arrive at different conclusion on these phenomena, is principally due to knowledge systems shaping their views in fundamental ways. This is the lens through which what they come to define as *truth* is viewed, defined and framed.

In research, paradigms are either explicitly declared or implicitly expressed. Ask your dissertation supervisor what their expectations and requirements are on this. In our own dissertation supervisor contexts we do recommend declaring one's paradigm alongside their metatheory in their dissertation as we strongly believe it is good research practice as, then, the reader will be in a position to appreciate what influences your work – particularly interpretations and conclusions. This will give your work a chance of being assessed from your paradigmatic viewpoint, rather than the marker's. It would be unideal to have your work misinterpreted. The onus is on you to ensure your work is as clear and understandable to the reader, in particular to the marker. Declaring your research paradigm is a good starting point. In social sciences, the dominant paradigms are *positivist*, *interpretivist* and *pragmatist*.

## 5.6.1 Positivist paradigm

The literature (e.g. Kivunja and Kuyini, 2017 and Bunge, 1996) attributes the introduction of the positivist paradigm to the French philosopher, Auguste Comte. Principal emphasis of the positivist paradigm is on what is considered scientific methodology which, in this context, emphasises "experimentation, observation and reason based on experience" (Kivunja and Kuyini, 2017:30). The positivist paradigm also assumes that *reality* is stable and, therefore, can be objectively defined (Levin, 1988). As such, this paradigm prioritises the use of quantitative measurement as a means to an *objective* end. Table 5.19 below, adapted from Kivunja and Kuyini (2017) and Bunge (1996), outlines underlying assumptions of the positivist paradigm.

*Table 5.18: Key positivist paradigm assumptions*

| |
|---|
| 1. All phenomena have cause and effect. |
| 2. Social phenomena are understood through observation or experimentation. |
| 3. Objectivity is the basis for understanding. |
| 4. Quantitative measurement is the only means to objective, verifiable social fact. |
| 5. Immeasurable, and therefore unverifiable, factors such as feelings, motives and purposes are fictions, not 'reality' or 'social fact'. |

There are, however, limitations to this paradigm. In table 5.19 below, we list some points the positivist paradigm overlooks.

*Table 5.19: Limitations of the positivist paradigm*

1. Not all phenomena have determinable cause and effect, particularly when other factors are not, or cannot be, controlled for.
2. Not all phenomena can be observed or experimented on. Most phenomena are too complex to understand just through observation and experimentation.
3. Absolute objectivity is almost impossible. At some point, subjectivity plays an important role in human understanding of phenomena, e.g. interpretation of results.
4. Not all phenomena can be quantitatively measured as they are too complex and too intricate to meaningfully measure quantitatively.
5. Putting pursuit of understanding of phenomena down to 'measurement' and 'verifiability' oversimplifies 'social fact'. Wholesome understanding of phenomena is a product of both the measurable and the immeasurable. Individual subjective experiences are as much *reality* as are 'measurable' and 'verifiable' phenomena.

## 5.6.2 Interpretivist/ Constructivist paradigm

The interpretivist paradigm is concerned with attempting to understand the subjective world of the human experience (Guba and Lincoln, 1989). In this respect, state Kivuja and Kuyini (2017), the perspective of the research participant is more important than that of the researcher. Therefore, any interpretation of the data collected should, as much as possible, be through the eyes of the participant or respondent. According to this viewpoint, *truth* and *reality* are a direct result of social agreement on their existence and meaning. They are socially constructed (hence *constructivist* paradigm or, simply, *constructivism*). From the same perspective, *truth* and *reality* are a product of collective social interpretations of their existence and meaning (hence *interpretivist* paradigm or *interpretivism*). In a research context, thus, interpretivism or constructivism views individual('s/s') constructions and interpretations of *truth* and *reality* as more important than researchers' constructions and interpretations. Hence, in research practice, all analyses, inferences, insights and claims to knowledge made in research findings, analyses, discussions, implications and recommendations should be supportable with primary qualitative data gathered. The main reason is that the participants' voice – hence their *interpretations* and *constructions* – are represented or captured in the primary data. Outside the participants' contextualised interpreted and constructed *truth* and *reality*, the two neither exist nor have meaning. So, any claims made without the backing of primary data are neither existent nor meaningful. It, therefore, makes sense that the interpretivist/ constructivist paradigm is aligned to qualitative research methods and methodologies. Table 5.20 below summarises core interpretivist/ constructivist paradigm assumptions.

*Table 5.20: Core interpretivist/ constructivist paradigm assumptions*

1. *Truth* and *reality* or *phenomena* are socially constructed.
2. *Truth* and *reality* or *phenomena* cannot exist, be studied or understood outside their 'natural' setting.
3. *Truth* and *reality* are subjective.
4. *Truth* and *reality* are not universal.
5. There are multiple *truths* and *realities* on any subject.
6. 'Natural' settings/ contexts give meaning and existence to *truth* and *reality*.
7. Individuals'/ research participants' viewpoints on phenomena or *truth* and *reality* being studied should be emphasised more than those of the researcher/ observer.

However, the interpretivist/ constructivist paradigm has its limitations. The main ones are outlined in table 5.21 below.

*Table 5.21: Limitations of the interpretivist/ constructivist paradigm*

| |
|---|
| 1. Overlooks universally occurring phenomena. |
| 2. Ignores consistency in meaning and understanding of certain phenomena. |
| 3. Results based on interpretivist research are difficult to generalise to other contexts outside the research setting. |
| 4. Makes it difficult to generate predictive theory as meaning is assumed to be confined to its 'natural' setting. |
| 5. It is difficult to draw 'meaningful' implications from interpretivist/ constructivist research as the 'natural' setting is assumed to give meaning and existence to phenomena or *truth* and *reality*. |

## 5.6.3 Pragmatist paradigm

The pragmatist paradigm seeks to address the main weaknesses of positivist and interpretivist paradigms by combining the strengths of these two. At the centre of pragmatism, which is attributed to the work of Dewey (1925), is the belief that pitting positivism and interpretivism against each other is unhelpful in the advancement of *knowledge* and the endeavour to make sense of constantly emerging *truth*, *reality* and *existence*. Pragmatism, posits Gabi (2015), is an attempt to acknowledge the value of singular and multiple *truths* and *realities* complementarity in research and general pursuit of *knowledge*, *truth* and *reality* (Creswell and Plano Clark, 2007; Rorty, 1999; Dewey, 1925; Rorty, 1999 and Feilzer, 2010). In keeping, of great importance to pragmatism is not whether *knowledge*, *truth* and *reality* are universalised or subjectivised. Rather, in accordance with Dewey (1925), emphasis is on whether this *knowledge*, *truth* and *reality* is sufficiently supportable or verifiable. In essence, anything can be 'made true' if verified (Dewey, 1925) hence being *pragmatic*. Therefore, pragmatism attaches value to combining positivism and interpretivism in making sense of phenomena. In essence, therein lies the relationship between pragmatism and the mixed-methods approach (Robson, 2002; Teddlie and Tashakkori, 2003 and 2006; Johnson and Onwuegbuzie, 2004). This enables the integrative research of phenomena without the dogmatic constraints of positivism and interpretivism – placing emphasis on justifiability of approach(es) rather than restrictive principles. Table 5.22 below lists the principal assumptions of the pragmatist paradigm.

*Table 5.22: Principal assumptions of the pragmatist paradigm*

1. *Knowledge, truth* and *reality* exists in both subjective and objective forms.

2. The 'full extent' of *knowledge, truth* and *reality* is realisable if both 'objective' and 'subjective' forms of *knowledge, truth* and *reality* are combined.

3. *Knowledge, truth* and *reality* are given credence or *existence* and *meaning* by their verifiability.

4. Sufficient supportability verifies *knowledge, truth* and *reality* or phenomena.

5. 'Subjective' and 'objective' *knowledge, truth* and *reality* exist in tandem with, rather than apart from, each other.

However, there are also limitations to the pragmatist paradigm, of which table 5.23 below gives the main ones.

*Table 5.23: Limitations or the pragmatist paradigm*

1. Oversimplifies 'subjective' and 'objective' *knowledge, truth* and *reality*.

2. Ignores some inherent contradictions between 'subjective' and 'objective' *knowledge, truth* and *reality*. 'Subjective' and 'objective' *knowledge, truth* and *reality* are not always complementary.

3. Verifiability, as it is inherently contingent on subjective interpretation, can be criticised for lack of objectivity – which undermines the assumed co-existence of 'subjective' and 'objective' *knowledge, truth* and *reality*.

4. Gives room to the flouting of research principles of systematic rigour and consistency in the guise on 'making anything true'.

## 5.7 Summary

The goal of this chapter was to explain and give guidance on some of the most commonly used methods and methodologies. We considered the meaning of the terms methods and methodologies and why it is important to distinguish between the two and, at the same time, appreciate the relationship thereof. We went on to provide a thick description and explanation of dominant qualitative, quantitative and mixed-methods designs. Appropriately, we ended by considering three main research paradigms – positivist, interpretivist and pragmatist. In relation to this, we, therefore, showed the links between research methods, methodologies and paradigm and how and why these need to be consistent with each other in any research design to enhance harmony and fluency. Building on this, the next chapter considers soundness of research – especially validity, reliability and Guba and Lincoln's (1985) alternative qualitative criteria.

# 6 SOUNDNESS: VALIDITY, RELIABILITY, QUALITATIVE CRITERIA

## 6.1 Overview

In research, the work's integrity rests almost entirely on the academic rigour with which it is carried out from its beginning to its ending. In this chapter, we attempt to address these critical research integrity issues and provide guidance on how best you can demonstrate that the integrity of your dissertation research is sound and, therefore, worthy at least a pass. We will begin by discussing the central research integrity points. Building on this, we will then consider dominant criteria for testing the soundness of an empirical study, specifically validity and reliability. Related to this, we also consider alternative criteria advanced by some qualitative researchers (based on the work of Guba and Lincoln, 1985). We then treat triangulation, epistemology, ontology and consistency. The summary highlights key points of this chapter.

## 6.2 Validity

Phelan and Wren (2005) define validity as the capacity of an instrument to measure what it is intended to measure. Focus here is on the extent to which results of a study represent what was studied. To this end, Robson (2002) posits that research findings should absolutely be what they appear to be about. In other words, valid findings neither exaggerate nor underreport what really emerged from a study. This speaks to the believability and trustworthiness of a study. A study is as significant as it is trustworthy and believable, otherwise there is no value to the work.

For the findings of your research to be academically significant, the work must be trustworthy. A study's thoroughness, from which it draws its trustworthiness, is dependent on how satisfactorily it addresses the central points. Trustworthiness also deals with six core elements detailed in table 6.1 below.

*Table 6.1: Testing the trustworthiness of your study*

**1. Does the research use the most appropriate methods for the study's context?**
- Use research methods consistent with research tradition in your field of study.
- Consider sample size.
- Data analysis methods and methodologies must be consistent with adopted data collection methods and methodologies. Analyse quantitative data quantitatively and qualitative data qualitatively.

**2. Are these methods used thoroughly?**
- Justify adopted methods
- Be systematic in your application of these methods.
- Show what you did, how and why.

**3. Is there sufficient attention to detail in the application of the research methods?**
- Avoid superficiality. Look at all the detail from all possible perspectives.
- For most research methods, there are specific phases which must be followed in the collection and analysis of data.

**4. Was the researcher open-minded in the collection of their data?**
- Do not get into a research context to prove. Rather, go to find out.
- Avoid bias.
- Do not allow your pre-conceived ideas or beliefs to influence the process and outcome of your research.

---

### 5. Is the data interpretation and analysis rounded and thorough?

- Interrogate your data thoroughly.
- Consider all possible, sometimes competing, interpretations of your data.
- e.g. "This finding possibly means … Another possible explanation could be … The extent of the impact of … cannot be conclusively determined as there are too many complex variables at play."

### 6. Are the conclusions contextually sensible?

- These are the 'therefores' of your study.
- Base your conclusions on the data and context of your research.
- e.g. "In light of the findings of this study, it would be reasonable to conclude that …. There are many conclusions that can be drawn from this study. The main ones are …".

---

*Adapted from Phelan and Wren (2005)*

In addition to these core elements, trustworthiness of your study will also be judged on the composition of your research instruments, in particular their key influences. Of principal interest here is whether the instruments are duly drawn from relevant core literature and the extent to which they are balanced.

Another question that will be raised regards data reduction. Research will almost always generate excessive data. This could be in excess of the focus and research questions of your investigation or in excess of the wordage of your dissertation. So, you are faced with having to reduce your data so that it fits with your purpose and research questions. Much care should be invested in how you arrive at using some of your data and not the other data. These decisions must be accounted for and justified. It would not be a good idea to carry out data reduction on expediency grounds such as personal preference for some findings to those excluded from your dissertation. Data reduction decisions can either enhance or harm the trustworthiness of your work. If wordage is a major constraint, we recommend you include some evidence of the soundness of your data reduction decisions in the appendices section of your dissertation. Be cautious enough to avoid confirmation bias, that is only selecting data which confirms one's preconceptions. You research to find out, not to prove. Next, let us briefly explore two main types of validity – internal and external.

## 6.2.1 Internal validity

Internal validity is driven by flaws within the research, for instance the design of the research instruments used in the study. For example, a poorly worded questionnaire (e.g. one asking leading questions) may generate responses which do not accurately represent the respondents' true perspectives on what the study actually purports to investigate. Furthermore, Seliger and Shohamy (1989:95) posit, "the interpretation of the data by the researcher ... [must be] clearly supportable" with data and, where possible, academically credible literature. If the research design and its instruments are flawed, the findings are fatally and incurably defective and, therefore, worthless.

## 6.2.2 External validity

External validity has to do with the question whether the findings of a study can be "...extended or applied to contexts outside those in which the research took place..." (Seliger and Shohamy, 1989:95). In your dissertation you will, in part, address this in the *implications* chapter or section. Again, this must be clearly supportable. It is advisable to say where the findings can be extended or applied and why you think this is so. Table 6.2 below outlines key factors affecting external validity you need to be mindful of in the conduct of your research.

*Table 6.2: Key factors affecting external validity*

### 1. Researcher influence

- These can either be conscious or unconscious biases on the topic.
- Researcher's failure to be open-minded.

### 2. Sample characteristics versus population characteristics

- If sample characteristics are inconsistent with those of the population, generalisations can be flawed.
- If there are inconsistences between your sample and the population it is drawn from, include caveats as to the generalisability of your findings. This can be included in the *limitations* section of your dissertation.

### 3. Effect of research environment

- In a dissertation context, the research environment is usually the setting where the data is collected.
- Severe restrictions on what can be studied, e.g. questions that can/ cannot be asked may limit your study's applicability.
- Strict restrictions on what can be reported in your dissertation could mean that the full extent of your core findings may never be known and, therefore, inapplicable and ungeneralizable.

### 4. Data collection methodology, i.e. data collection process

- Inappropriate data collection methodology, e.g. conducting a questionnaire survey on a sample of five or carrying out 1000 interviews. This negatively impacts on analysability and interpretability of the data collected.
- Sometimes the actual process, even if the method is appropriate, can be defective.

### 5. The effect of time, dispensation or season on respondents

- When a study is carried out is also important, and can influence the generalisability of your findings.
- e.g. Researching stress among GCSE students during an exams period will likely return high stress results compared to if the study was undertaken during a non-exam period.

## 6.3 Reliability

In accordance with Phelan and Wren (2005), reliability is the capacity of an instrument to result in consistent results. Say you get onto a scale five times in quick succession, and you get widely varied readings to the point that you are no longer sure how much exactly you weigh. That scale can be said to be unreliable. Similarly, your research instruments or measures must produce stable and consistent results if all other factors in the deployment of the instruments are constant. This has to do with consistency and repeatability of your measures. Because complex and intricate factors are involved, reliability is inexact and, therefore, almost impossible to calculate in precise terms. To address this in a dissertation, focus more on the consistency of design and application of your instruments or measures. Table 6.3 below gives you further guidance on how you should test your research's reliability.

*Table 6.3: Types of reliability tests*

---

### 1. Inter-Observer Reliability
- To assess the degree to which different observers give consistent estimates of the same phenomenon.

### 2. Test-Retest Reliability
- To assess consistency of a measure from one time to another.

### 3. Parallel-Forms Reliability
- To assess consistency of the results of two tests constructed in the same way from the same content domain. i.e. Different versions of the same instrument

### 4. Internal Consistency Reliability
- To assess the consistency of results across items within a test

---

*Source: Web Center for Social Research Methods (2017: online)*

There are also key sources of unreliability you need to be mindful of during the conduct of your research as presented by the Web Center for Social Research Methods (2017) and Robson (2002). Please see table 6.4 below.

*Table 6.4: Sources of unreliability*

---

### 1. Participant error
- Fatigue could lead to rushed completion of a questionnaire. i.e. not a true reflection of an individual's perspectives.

### 2. Participant bias
- e.g. eagerness to please could influence a participant's responses.

### 3. Observer error
- e.g. the researcher carried out observation when they were too tired

### 4. Construct validity
- e.g. Item/ question means different things to participant from what it means to you?

---

## 6.4 Alternative qualitative criteria

While validity and reliability are the widely used criteria for determining the integrity of a study, some dominant qualitative research proponents object to, reject even, the application of these frameworks to qualitative research as, according to them, the frameworks are significantly skewed towards quantitative studies. In their rejection of reliability and validity frameworks, they present multiple reasons why the frameworks do not work and, therefore, should not be used in qualitative research. The main arguments are outlined in table 6.5 below.

*Table 6.5: Arguments for the rejection of reliability and validity frameworks in qualitative research*

- Truth and reality are subjective.
- Therefore, truth cannot be exactly determinable.
- Truth and reality are relative and, therefore, unrepeatable.

In keeping with these arguments, dominant qualitative researchers argue that there should be alternative standards for judging the soundness of research. Over the years, one alternative set of criteria that has gained traction in its application in research are Guba and Lincoln's (1985) criteria in table 6.6 below.

*Table 6.6: Guba and Lincoln's (1985) four criteria*

| Traditional Criteria | Alternative Criteria |
|---|---|
| Internal validity | **Credibility**<br>• Believability from participant's view |
| External validity | **Transferability**<br>• To what extent are the results transferrable to other contexts? |
| Reliability | **Dependability**<br>• The need for the research to account for changes occurring in the setting. |
| Objectivity | **Confirmability**<br>• To what extent can the results be confirmed by others? |

## 6.5 Triangulation

Triangulation refers to "…the use of **more than one** approach…" (Heale and Forbes, 2013:98) in researching a topic. This includes **methodology triangulation, theory triangulation** and **investigator** or **researcher triangulation** (Hertfordshire University, 2017). **Methodology triangulation** refers to using more than one research method in a single study. **Theory triangulation** means utilising more than one theory to make sense of the research. **Investigator** or

**researcher triangulation** is using more than one researcher in the same study. You can employ any of these types of triangulation to enhance the soundness of your study. You do not have to restrict yourself to one type of triangulation. For example, you can use one research method and employ a range of theoretical approaches to interpret your findings and still sufficiently satisfy the triangulation criterion. It is advisable that, in your dissertation, you specify what type of triangulation you adopt, how and why.

*Table 6.7: Types of triangulation*

**1. Methodology triangulation**
- Using more than one research method in a single study.
- e.g. Mixed-methods research.

**2. Theory triangulation**
- Utilising more than one theory to make sense of a phenomenon.
- Interpreting findings from competing theoretical perspectives.

**3. Investigator or researcher triangulation**
- More than one researcher involved in a single study.
- Researchers can then compare findings and attempt to arrive at balanced interpretations and conclusions.

## 6.6 Ontology and epistemology

**Ontology** concerns itself with **what it is that constitutes reality** (Scotland, 2012). In your dissertation, you should be clear what it is that will constitute reality in the context of your research topic, focus and research questions. In other words, what specific elements of the topic do you intend to collect data on that will enable you with claims of and to reality?

**Epistemology** refers to **what you know, how you come to know it and how valid it is** (Koro-Ljungberg, Yendol-Hoppey, Smith and Hayes, 2009). By now you should be aware that knowledge and truth are subjective and relative. In an academic context, particularly in research, the underlying assumption is that valid knowledge and truth are underpinned by a theory knowledge which shapes individuals' view of reality. Therefore, one's epistemology influences their paradigmatic and data collection and analysis methodology decisions.

There is, therefore, a link between ontology and epistemology. Ontology (i.e. what reality is) and epistemology (i.e. what we know about this reality and how we come to know it) interact and, subsequently, influence our claims to knowledge. For your dissertation research, you need to be clear which reality you are going to study (ontology) and how it is going to be studied (epistemology).

There is a plethora of epistemologies and ontologies identified in the literature (e.g. Koro-Ljungberg, Yendol-Hoppey, Smith and Hayes, 2009). Some of these are objectivism, subjectivism, constructionism, contextualism, empiricism, feminist epistemology, relativism and hybrid epistemologies. It is important to note that ontology and epistemology generally share labels. The labels are then defined from both ontological and epistemological standpoints.

*Table 6.8: Links between epistemologies, paradigms and research methods*

| Ontologies and Epistemologies | Paradigms | Research methods |
|---|---|---|
| **1. Objectivism**<br>• Concerned with 'facts'<br>• Facts exist independent of people or social entities. | • Positivism | • Quantitative |
| **2. Subjectivism**<br>• Social phenomena are created from perceptions and resultant actions.<br>• Reality and truth are subjective. | • Interpretivism<br>• Pragmatism | • Qualitative<br>• Mixed-methods |
| **3. Constructionism**<br>• Also known as social constructionism. | • Interpretivism<br>• Pragmatism | • Qualitative<br>• Mixed-methods |

| | | |
|---|---|---|
| • Reality is socially constructed.<br>• Individuals perceive situations differently. | | |
| **4. Contextualism**<br>• Also known as epistemic contextualism (EC).<br>• Knowledge attribution is dependent on the attributor's context.<br>• Phenomena will take different meanings in different contexts. | • Interpretivism<br>• Pragmatism | • Qualitative<br>• Mixed-methods |
| **5. Empiricism**<br>• Knowledge is dependent upon sense experience.<br>• e.g. visual, hearing, touch experience | • Positivism<br>• Interpretivism<br>• Pragmatism | • Quantitative<br>• Qualitative<br>• Mixed-methods |
| **6. Feminist epistemology**<br>• Holds that dominant conceptions and practices of knowledge disadvantage women.<br>• Argues that gender should influence how knowledge is conceived. | • Interpretivism<br>• Pragmatism | • Qualitative<br>• Mixed-methods |
| **7. Relativism**<br>• Truth and falsity are not universal.<br>• Truth and falsity depend on standards and ways of reasoning and justification.<br>• Cultural norms and individual standards are key to what is | • Interpretivism<br>• Pragmatism | • Qualitative<br>• Mixed-methods |

| | | |
|---|---|---|
| considered true and valid. | | |
| **8. Hybrid epistemologies**<br>▪ Valid knowledge is contingent on the interaction between, and combination of, various, complementary ways of knowing.<br>▪ No single form of knowing is privileged over another. | ▪ Pragmatism | ▪ Mixed-methods |

Drawn from the literature on research epistemology.

## 6.7 Consistency: Keeping harmony within the study

One of the major challenges in dissertation work is maintaining consistency between the different intricately linked components of what constitutes this emerging major work at this level of study. In particular, there must be mutual consistency between the research topic, research aim and questions, paradigm, research methods (both data collection and analysis), recommendations for further study and conclusions. Expressed briefly, there must be consistency between what you do and what you write (across all chapters of the dissertation). For instance, if you adopt the mixed-methods approach, then your research paradigm should be pragmatism. Analysis for such a study should be integrative, that is combining quantitative and qualitative analysis methodologies. The literature review should draw on quantitative, qualitative and mixed-methods studies. In addition, the literature review should be relevant to the research questions. Essentially, research questions should influence all chapters of your dissertation. Anything that is irrelevant to these research questions should not be included in the dissertation.

Another important aspect of consistency is register or voice used. Decide whether you will write in the first or third person. Some research supervisors will insist on voice consistency, rather than switching between first and third-person voices. However, we have seen some sound, well-written work which fluently, appropriately and effectively switches between voices, without undermining the flow of the writing. Thus, our advice in this regard is that you should find out what the expectations are within your department. Some of these issues come down to supervisor preferences. Because they will be marking your work, we strongly recommend you follow your supervisor's guidance as they will likely mark how they will have guided you.

## 6.8 Summary

The soundness of your work is central, not only to the grade you will attain, but also to whether your work will pass in the first place. When markers have read your work, the key question they will want to satisfy themselves on has to do with the integrity of the work. Validity and reliability or – if following stringent qualitative arguments – credibility, transferability, dependability and confirmability are an absolute requirement insofar as attesting the integrity of your work is concerned. These need to be treated with much rigour and care to ensure consistency and appropriateness of decisions, approaches and findings. Being rigorous means sufficiently demonstrating what you did, how you did it and why you did it the way you did it. What you did refers to the research techniques. How you did it are the methodologies, that is the processes of putting the methods into action. The *why* is a concoction of justification premises, including ontology and epistemology, and links to research tradition in your research field. Linked to soundness of research is the appropriateness of the topic and processes for the selected participants. This is the question on whether research has been conducted in an ethical manner, which is the subject of the next chapter.

# 7 ETHICAL CONSIDERATIONS

## 7.1 Overview

At its core, social science research is intended to peel off, layer by layer, what can be considered a knowledge onion. With each layer, there are further discoveries, enhanced understandings, new skills, intrigues and surprises with, hopefully, some positive outcomes emerging from the effort. Because almost all social research is done with or affects humans, there is need to ensure that no negative effect or harm – physical, emotional, psychological or otherwise – is done during the process of the study, and that human dignity is upheld at all times.

Academic departments will insist on your study gaining ethical approval before you proceed with your research. This is to ensure that the proposed study satisfactorily fulfils all ethical expectations. Besides determining the effect of your study on its participants, a further consideration is the research's impact on you. This is to ensure your personal, academic and professional integrity and interests are protected. In this chapter, the main goal is to equip you with some of the most common ethical issues surrounding research with humans. It is our hope that you will be able to then contextualise these ethical issues to your own study.

This chapter begins by illuminating on the meanings of ethics in general, and how these can influence the meaning and understandings of ethics in the context of research. Next, expanding on understandings of ethics, is a discussion on ethical principles and their implications for conducting social science research. The third section provides practical guidance on identifying and addressing ethical issues for your research. A summary of the key points of this chapter is provided in the conclusion.

## 7.2 What are ethics?

The literature on social science research provides a range of divergent and convergent positions on the meaning of ethics. In the next subsection we look at the principal understandings of this term and attempt to give an operational definition which will be adopted in the present work.

### 7.2.1 Defining ethics

The term ethics carries varying meanings in different contexts and to different people. As such, it is unsurprising that researchers will conceive it divergently to each other. Loubert (1999:162) describes ethics as "rules, standards and principles that dictate right conduct ... based on moral values". In the context of research, McNamee and Bridges (2002) identify access and consent, voice and empowerment, virtue and conflict – among others – as the most central pillars of the ethics construct. Thus, we will operationalise the definition of ethics as rules, standards and principles governing the conduct and dissemination of research, principally safety, access and consent, confidentiality, voice and empowerment, conflict, participation and integrity.

### 7.2.2 Universalisation of ethics

There has often been debate on the contextual nature of ethics, how they vary from place to place and across research. As such, agreeing on what can be considered ethical in an absolute sense is not exactly an objective to pursue. That said, from the various perspectives on ethics (e.g. Loubert, 1999 and McNamee and Bridges, 2002), it can be inferred that some general features commonly applied in research exist. Drawing on the operational definition above, these have to do with safety, access and consent, confidentiality, voice and empowerment, conflict and participation and integrity.

### 7.2.3 Safety and wellbeing

Safety and wellbeing is, arguably, the most important of the core ethical considerations, especially as humans are usually involved in the conduct of social research. Here, safety can be conceived on two dimensions – physical and psychological. In this respect, it is worth noting that, besides the safety and wellbeing of your participants, your safety and wellbeing – as the researcher – should also be taken into consideration. The nature and process of the research project should be such that it does not cause harm, or put at risk of harm, participants and researchers during the course of the research. As highlighted, safety and wellbeing should be looked at more broadly than just the physical domain. The Social Research Association's (2018:1) *Code of Practice for the Safety of Social Researchers* outlines core considerations in table 7.1 below.

*Table 7.1: Core ethical considerations*

---

**1. Risk of physical threat or abuse**
- Plan for safety in research design.
- Carry out risk assessment.
- Your research must be such that it does not put you or your participants at risk of physical threat or abuse.
- It is important to consider the safety record of the research setting and participants.
- Consider the physical and contextual environment.

**2. Risk of psychological trauma, as a result of actual or threatened violence or the nature of what is disclosed during the interaction**
- Carry out risk assessment.
- Consider the topic, particularly the scope of the subject and nature of questions to be asked.
- If engaging in sensitive research, consider the limits of what can be covered for purposes of the study.
- Think carefully if, for certain topics, it might be a good idea to research third-party perspectives if your target participants are particularly emotionally or psychologically vulnerable.

---

**3. Risk of being in a compromising situation, in which there might be accusations of improper behaviour.**
- Carry out risk assessment.
- Clarify responsibilities.
- It is always best practice to carry out research in appropriate locations where both you and the participant are comfortable.
- If your research involves children or vulnerable adults, it is best research practice to carry out the study in the presence of an observer or in an open space.

**4. Increased exposure to risks of everyday life and social interaction, such as road accidents and infectious illness.**
- Carry out risk assessment.
- Clarify responsibilities.
- Your physical safety is also of paramount importance.
- Ensure the physical environment is safe and does not put you at the risk of infectious illness.

**5. Risk of causing psychological or physical harm to others.**
- Carry out risk assessment.
- Clarify responsibilities.
- Your conduct as a researcher should not be such that there is risk of inflicting psychological or physical harm on others.
- Avoid an intimidating demeanour.
- Avoid questions which may be deemed psychologically harmful.
- Do not ask respondents to carry out potentially harmful activities.

## 7.2.4 Access and consent

Without access and consent, there is no research. Negotiating and gaining access and consent should, however, still be carried out in an appropriate manner. One of the core values surrounding this is honesty and integrity on the part of the researcher. In respect of this, avoid gaining access and consent dishonestly or in a way that can be construed as deceitful. Ensure that you disclose all the core elements of your study, for example what the research is on, what it involves, how long it will take and how the results will be reported and disseminated. Alongside this, it is also appropriate to inform the setting and participants of their rights in the context of the research. What this means, broadly, is that for settings to give you access, and participants consent, they must be sufficiently informed. In the absence of this, any access and consent given are void. Therefore, neither withhold nor exaggerate information about your research.

## 7.2.5 Confidentiality

Data collected in the course of your research must not be reported in a way that is traceable to the individual participants or their settings. At the same time, avoid using actual names of participants or their settings. Instead, use pseudonyms to protect individual and setting identities.

However, there often appears to be conflation of confidentiality and absolute secrecy. In the context of ethics in research, the two do not mean the same. In most legal jurisdictions, there are circumstances where identities of individuals or settings ought to be disclosed. For instance, if a crime has been disclosed in the course of your research, you may find yourself in a position whereby you will be expected to report this to the relevant people. Who to report this to will depend on rules and policies of the particular setting in which you will be conducting your study. The same will apply if a participant discloses to you that they have been a victim of an alleged crime or abuse. While these instances are rare in social research, it is important that you do not promise absolute secrecy to settings and participants. Rather, guarantee confidentiality – which means that information will only be shared on a need-to-know basis. Again, check what the laws, rules and regulations are in your specific country and context.

## 7.2.6 Voice and empowerment

Voice and empowerment have to do with free expression and autonomy participants are accorded during the course of your research. Ethically, even though this is your research, it is appropriate to listen to the voice of your participants regarding the extent and nature of their participation. For example, they may have a preferred time and venue. As long as these are appropriate, you should allow your participants these choices. Additionally, participants may not be comfortable answering certain questions. Again, you should take this into consideration and empower participants to express their preferences. In some cases, participants may choose to withdraw their participation before or during the study. Where this happens, participants do not have an obligation to tell you why they are withdrawing and should not have any penalties imposed on them as a result, neither should they be victimised or pressurised to keep participating against their freewill.

## 7.2.7 Conflict

Undertaking a research project with humans can sometimes present sources of conflict. Some of these can emanate from role conflict. For example, having dual roles such as employee and researcher – if you are going to conduct your study in your workplace – will likely lead to some dilemmas. These could be whether what you wish to have access to as a researcher could be off bounds to your professional role. This could result in some limits being imposed on the extent of access you will be given. Some of these limits could have significant ramifications on your ability to meet your research aims or on the capacity of your study to address your research questions.

Another challenge could be if you intend to conduct research in your child's school and, in the process, have access to other parents' children. Some parents may be too reticent to allow you to access their children in school. Awareness of such undercurrents will help you prepare ways of navigating potential conflict, especially when your participants are too vulnerable to reasonably give their own informed consent. This is one of the reasons why full disclosure is important when seeking access, in order to give gatekeepers an opportunity to genuinely give informed consent. Taking this step will help prevent potential future conflict emanating from your study.

While it is to be expected that researchers will likely avoid causing or being involved in conflict, sometimes such situations will arise during the course of your research. If you happen to be caught up in such a scenario, it is advisable to keep gatekeepers and your research supervisor fully informed so that appropriate support and guidance can be offered. Depending on what it is and its gravity, gatekeepers and dissertation supervisors will be in a position to determine if the situation can be resolved or if you need to leave the setting and seek to carry on with your research somewhere different. That said, as far as you have control over a situation, try not to be a source of conflict yourself. Your position as a researcher is much easier to handle if conflict is coming from elsewhere, not you. It is always important to handle yourself with integrity as your and your institution's reputations will be at stake.

## 7.2.8 Participation and integrity

Participation and integrity also have a significant impact on participants. Participation primarily has to do with the level and nature of respondent involvement in the research process while integrity refers to how this process makes them feel, specifically with respect to their self-worth. What you ask participants to do as part of your research should not undermine their sense of self-worth. As far as is possible, avoid asking questions which leave your participants humiliated or patronised. Use appropriate language and, if you will ask research participants to carry out certain activities as part of your study, avoid activities which may be considered inappropriate in the context of the setting in which you will be doing your research. This further highlights the importance of close consultation with your research supervisor for guidance on what is considered appropriate or acceptable in respect to what you propose to do in your study before carrying it out. If in doubt, it is always important to ask, as opposed to risking infringing on ethical expectations. In addition, there is also need to clarify roles and responsibilities beforehand so that all parties are clear what is involved and if they wish to proceed to take part.

Also be clear on what your research participants' rights are. However, it is important to note that there will likely be context-specific rights and obligations in addition to the somewhat generic or broader rights you will have anticipatorily taken into consideration at the planning stage of your research process. Therefore, even when you have covered the participant rights aspect at planning, from an ethical standpoint, you will still need to further clarify context-specific issues regarding participant rights and obligations – especially in formal settings such as schools. Some formal settings will likely have strict guidelines and restrictions regarding research participation within them. They may have limits on what topics research in these may not cover, which is why it is of paramount importance to be clear on your research aims and processes at access negotiation stage. Should you fundamentally change aspects of your research, for example questions you will ask in interviews, it is good practice to discuss these changes with your dissertation supervisor and research setting gatekeepers. This will protect you, your institution and your participants. If you keep your dissertation supervisor updated on your dissertation process, you will put yourself in a position to get timely guidance on research decision-making.

## 7.2.9 Determining an ethical issue

Another question most students ask is how one determines their research ethical issue. On this, we tend to call attention to the nebulous nature of ethics as these tend to be somewhat non-fixed. They are difficult to universalise, especially so when our readers are from a range of very diverse countries and contexts. Notwithstanding, the following questions will help in considering the ethical issues of your research.

*Table 7.2: Determining ethical issues for your research*

| |
|---|
| **1. Who?** |
|     ▪ This refers to the people who will be affected by your research. |
|     ▪ Who will be your participants? |
|     ▪ How vulnerable are they to processes and outcomes of your research? |
|     ▪ How can you protect them from, or mitigate their vulnerability to, your research? |
|   |
| **2. What?** |
|     ▪ What are the aims of your research? |
|     ▪ Are these aims morally acceptable in your context? |
|     ▪ What are the processes of your research? What does this research involve? |
|     ▪ Is any aspect of what your research intends to achieve, and the process thereof, morally appropriate? |

- What aspects of your study may potentially expose those involved in it to harm (this can be physical, psychological or other – again, depending on context)?

## 3. Where?
- This mostly covers, although it is not limited to, the research setting.
- Be aware of moral expectations, traditions and standards of where you will conduct your study.
- Different settings have different sensitivities, and you must be aware of these before you begin your study. For example, in some children's settings it is inappropriate to use photography as one of your data collection approaches.
- Settings will also have different rules on a range of aspects. For instance, use of mobile phones or any voice recording equipment may be prohibited in high-security contexts like prisons.

## 4. When?
- This has to do with timing.
- Knowing **when** certain research processes or activities are appropriate is as important as knowing **what** is acceptable.
- The appropriateness of certain actions, activities and processes is time-bound. What is appropriate at one time may not be appropriate at another time.
- In some cases, something is considered appropriate as long as it does not exceed its time limit. It is important to be aware how long is acceptable period of your time to carry out your research. Know when to start. Know when to finish.
- Intervals may be important for certain settings. For example, some settings may stipulate that you do not stay in them for longer than one hour per visit at fortnightly intervals. This is sometimes so the disruption of your research process to the setting's core activities is minimised.

## 5. How?
- This refers to your research process or processes.
- How you conduct your research may expose participants to potential harm.

- Some participants or settings may have preferences on or limits to how research is conducted.
- Considering how, particularly methodologies, your research will be conducted will help you identify potential ethical considerations before you start.

## 6. Why?

- These are reasons why you are conducting your research.
- For some settings and participants, reasons behind a research activity are important and may be a key determinant in their decision to participate.
- Even though some participants or settings may be happy with what the study involves, they may be uncomfortable with why it is being carried out.
- Do you have a morally acceptable reason for carrying out your research? The best way to find out would be to share your research aim with your dissertation supervisor in the first instance, and with the participants and setting before you begin.

## 7. Therefore?

- This has to do with the outcome. It is the *so what?*
- In light of the above considerations, can your study morally proceed as it is, with amendments or not.
- This also refers to the outcome of your study.
- What is the end goal of the research outcome?
- Who is exposed to physical or psychological harm as a result of the outcome of your study?
- Also consider how results of the study will be disseminated.
- Share this with your dissertation supervisor, setting gatekeepers and, if appropriate, participants.

## 7.3 Social research ethical principles

Depending on country and context, ethical principles will likely vary. Even so, the core features – especially the essence – of these principles will likely be similar. We especially find the Economic and Social

Research Council (ESRC) (2018) six core principles listed below useful as a guide on the ethical conduct of research.

*Table 7.3: ESRC's six key principles for ethical research*

**1. Research should aim to maximise benefit for individuals and society and minimise risk and harm**

- Besides the fact that you intend to use your research for your academic benefit, consider and spell out its benefit to participants and society.

**2. The rights and dignity of individuals and groups should be respected**

- Be aware of your participants' contextual rights and dignity issues and respect them.

**3. Wherever possible, participation should be voluntary and appropriately informed**

- Sufficiently and appropriately informed participation is better than participation based on insufficient information. Provide sufficient enough information for participants to make informed choices and decisions on taking part in your research.
- Unless the study is mandatory or statutory, all research participation must be voluntary.
- Avoid coercing participants into taking part in your study.

**4. Research should be conducted with integrity and transparency**

- Honesty, truthfulness, veracity and reliability are integral pillars of ethical research. Ensure your conduct throughout the lifecycle of your research abundantly reflects these qualities.
- Provide sufficient information on your research process to all stakeholders. These include participants, settings and, up to a point, your dissertation supervisor.
- Give your participants and settings the ability to obtain information pertaining to your research when they need it (Ball, 2009).

**5. Lines of responsibility and accountability should be clearly defined**
- In the context of your research, where everyone's responsibility and accountability begin and ends should be clarified and adhered to. This minimises doubt and disquiet.
- You also need to know where your responsibility and accountability begin and end. If in doubt, ask your research supervisor before you begin the research process.

**6. Independence of research should be maintained and where conflicts of interest cannot be avoided, they should be made explicit**
- Research should not be unduly influenced, to the extent of being biased or untrustworthy. Rather carry it out independently so that its findings' integrity is not undermined.
- Consider carefully if there is any conflict of interest, e.g. researching on your professional practice which may reveal your professional shortcomings.

## 7.4 Summary

Ethics in research remain an important feature throughout the lifecycle of a study. They influence if a study will be carried out and, if so, how. It is, therefore, incumbent on the researcher that they are aware of ethical issues surrounding their research topic, the setting in which the study will be conducted and the broader context, such as the country, where the study is undertaken. Awareness and consideration of ethical issues will assist in getting your research approved before you begin. Beyond that, it is worth noting that ethics do not end at approval of your topic. If anything, that is where they begin. Thus, ethics ought to be adhered to throughout the lifecycle of the research.

The purpose of this chapter was to illuminate core ethical issues related to research with humans. Among other things, we considered how complex and non-fixed research ethical considerations are and their tendency to be ongoing for the lifecycle of the investigation. As much as this non-fixity and non-universality is an existent feature of ethics in social research, we argued that – at their core – ethical principles are underpinned by a common broad objective of upholding integrity and fairness during the lifecycle of the research project by protecting the moral interests of all stakeholders of that study. With this in mind, it is also important to take into consideration contextual ethical factors, some of which may be influenced by timing. In the next chapter, focus shifts to data analysis methods and methodologies.

# 8 DATA ANALYSIS METHODS AND METHODOLOGIES

## 8.1 Overview

Data analysis essentially refers to an attempt to make sense of the data. This could involve identifying overarching patterns within and across datasets and establishing what these patterns mean and their implications in the context of the study conducted. This chapter sets out to explore qualitative, quantitative and mixed-methods data analysis approaches. We also provide useful examples of how data may be analysed. The chapter further acknowledges the complexities of data analysis and the extent of subjective interpretation, hence the need for the researcher to practice self-reflexivity which is about constantly asking yourself why you are choosing to 'see' and make sense of phenomena in this/ these way(s). This involves becoming conscious of influences that are rooted in your own history, culture and how these influence your perceptions of participants' realities. Thus, your data analysis, interpretation and writing process should seek to re-examine, re-consider and re-contextualise the fieldwork experience and its entanglement with personal experiences. We then provide guidance on how to identify and acknowledge your study's limitations as this then helps you connect these limitations with suggestions for further research.

As you may have gathered your data from diverse sources, the analysis process will help you interrogate the data in order to gain insights that are actionable. You will need to consider your paradigmatic positioning and how this relates to the way you analyse and interpret the data. This helps the reader appreciate how you are making sense of your study. It is also important to consider your analytical framework. Different frameworks are consistent with different 'ways of knowing' or epistemic frameworks/ epistemology. Remember, your analytical framework is the window through which your reader will access your study. Thus, the analytical framework is as important as your paradigm and the way(s) in which you conceptualise the subject or topic. A particular study could be articulated and presented in diverse ways.

The Academy for Educational Development (2006:15) conceptualises data analysis as a flexible cyclical approach (figure 8.1) which accommodates varying decision-making processes.

*Figure 8.1: Cyclical approach to data analysis*

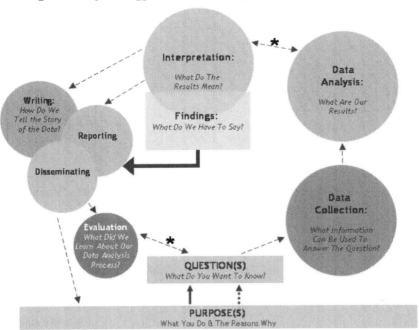

*Source: The Academy for Educational Development (2006)*

## 8.2 Qualitative data analysis approaches

There are a range of qualitative data analysis approaches you may want to consider. Before you select a relevant data analysis approach for your study, you will need to familiarise with your data in order to identify key themes that are emerging from it. In relation to the Academy for Educational Development (2006) diagram (figure 8.1 above), think about what your results are and what they might mean in relation to your research questions, and how you are going to tell the story or present your findings.

### 8.2.1 Discourse analysis

Discourse analysis explores sets of ideas and meanings that are constructed by language and how these create power. There are different approaches to discourse analysis. Table 8.1, drawn from Williams and O'Connor (2017), illustrates discourse analysis approaches and their foci.

*Table 8.1: Discourse analysis approaches*

| Approach to Discourse analysis | Focus of analysis |
|---|---|
| Discursive Psychology | How is language constructed, situated in interaction and bound up with actions |
| Critical Discourse Analysis (CDA) | The role language plays in establishing and perpetuating dominance and power in society |
| Foucauldian Discourse Analysis | A historical analysis of language; examining rules, divisions, and systems associated with a particular body of knowledge. |

### 8.2.2 Content analysis

Content analysis is "…a procedure for the categorisation of verbal or behavioural data, for purposes of classification, summarisation and tabulation…" (University of Surrey, 2016: online). This approach relates to quantitative data analysis.

## 8.2.3 Thematic analysis

Thematic analysis is probably the most dominant qualitative data analysis methodology. Besides, most other qualitative data analysis approaches are drawn from thematic analysis and, therefore, broadly mimic this analysis approach, albeit with some minor modifications. Therefore, it is appropriate to devote more attention to this analysis process.

According to Braun and Clarke (2006:4), thematic analysis involves "...identifying, analysing and reporting patterns (themes) within data ...". These authors offer a six-step thematic analysis process which we draw on in our condensed version of their model in table 8.2.

*Table 8.2: Thematic analysis phases*

---

**1. Familiarising with your data:**
   - Transcribing
   - Reading and annotating

**2. Categorising your annotations**
   - Sort identified themes into broad categories or cluster

**3. Identifying themes**
   - Assign descriptive labels to the categories or clusters.
   - What story does each cluster or category tell? Try to express this in one sentence per category or cluster?
   - What is the best theme that represents each category or cluster?

**4. Identifying links between themes**
   - Try to make connection between the themes identified in 3 above.
   - What is the nature of each connection or link? Some links could be contradictory. Others might be causal. But there are more link types you will likely find. These are not prescriptive.

---

---

**5. Theme reduction**

- If you discover you have too many themes to analyse within the scope of your dissertation, consider reducing them. You may want to use your research questions to do this.

---

*Adapted from Braun and Clarke (2006)*

*Figure 8.2: Example of an annotated transcript*

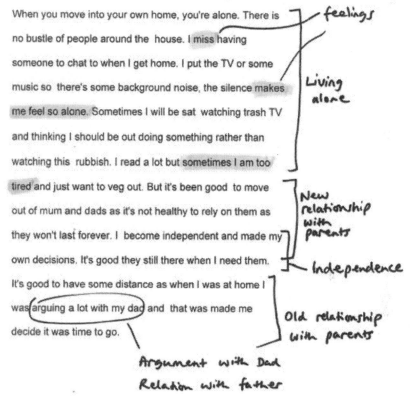

*Source: University of Huddersfield (2017: Online)*

*Figure 8.3: Example of an annotated transcript with some links identified*

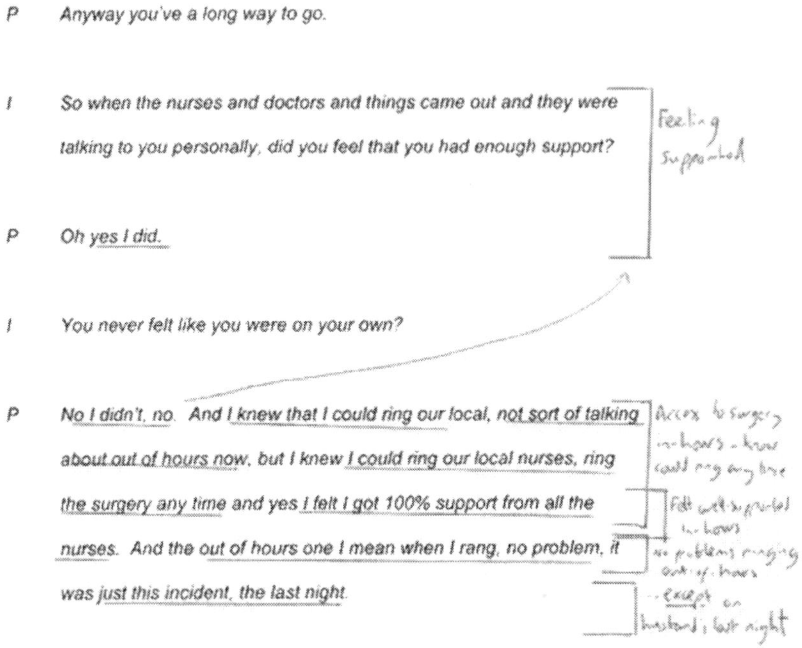

P      Anyway you've a long way to go.

I      So when the nurses and doctors and things came out and they were

talking to you personally, did you feel that you had enough support?    Feeling Supported

P      Oh yes I did.

I      You never felt like you were on your own?

P      No I didn't, no. And I knew that I could ring our local, not sort of talking

about out of hours now, but I knew I could ring our local nurses, ring

the surgery any time and yes I felt I got 100% support from all the

nurses. And the out of hours one I mean when I rang, no problem, it

was just this incident, the last night.

*Source: University of Huddersfield (2018: Online)*

When you have collected your data, you will need to read and annotate it in order to identify key emerging themes. As noted by Dey (1993) annotating is an enhancement to reflective reading on the research questions (i.e. purposive reading). During this stage, you will begin to probe the data as if you have not collected it in first place. In a way you will be attempting to create a distance between you and the data and begin to ask such questions as: What is the data about? What story does it tell? This approach will enable you to look at the data with an 'open' mind. That said, it is not completely easy to distance yourself from the data you have collected. This is where you will need to consider how you have positioned yourself paradigmatically. It is important to also consider the underlying philosophical assumptions about what constitutes your research and how knowledge is developed. If you are approaching your data from an interpretivist paradigm for example, you will need to consider multiple truths and realities that exist and your participants' subjective experiences in relation to your chosen focus.

Annotations on field notes and interview transcript will then help you come up with major categories around which subcategories may be built. After establishing links between categories and subcategories which will help develop your analysis. Creating categories helps to identify key themes from your data. An example below from a study which examined the role of play in learning and teaching illustrates the process:

*Table 8.3: Example of data categorisation*

| Categories | Evidence from the data |
|---|---|
| Compatibility of play and learning | <ul><li>Teacher's belief in *compatibility* of play and learning.</li><li>Children's belief in *incompatibility* of play and learning.</li><li>Observation of children in the presence and absence of the teacher.</li></ul> |
| Perception of play | <ul><li>Teacher's definition and perception.</li><li>Pupils' contrasting views on play.</li><li>Pupil's pictures of places they enjoy playing in.</li></ul> |
| Use of play | <ul><li>Observations of teacher mixing learning with play.</li><li>Observations of pupils during lessons.</li><li>Observations of pupils during break times.</li></ul> |
| Gender differences in play | <ul><li>Observations of pupils during break times.</li><li>Observations of teacher-allocation of play activities among children.</li></ul> |
| Misconception of play by other teachers | <ul><li>Teacher's view (in the interview) that some teachers need to be informed on the importance of play.</li></ul> |

*Figure 8.4: Establishing links between and across categories*

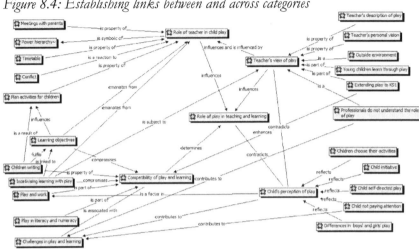

Below, we give further examples of how links can be illustrated across themes based on Gabi's (2006) work.

*Figure 8.5: Example of thematic links*

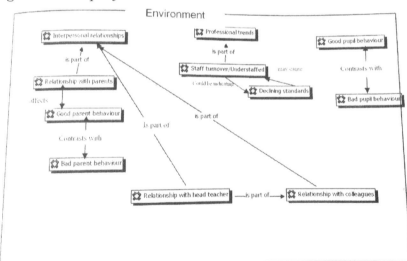

*Figure 8.6: Example of personality qualities thematic links*

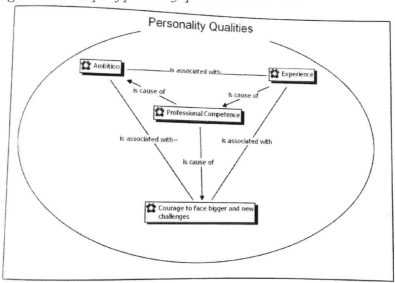

*Figure 8.7: Example of professional roles thematic links*

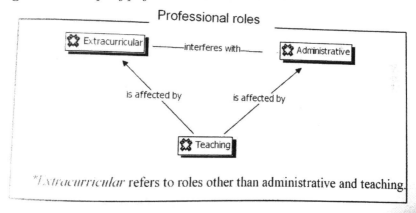

*Figure 8.8: Example of theme reduction and/ compacting*

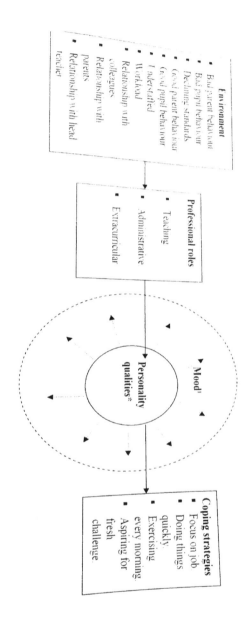

## 8.3 Quantitative data analysis

Quantitative data can be analysed in multiple ways, depending on research purpose and questions. These numerous ways fall under two broad types of data analysis, that is descriptive and inferential statistical analyses. Descriptive data analysis is primarily about summarising and exploring patterns (Agresti and Finlay, 1997) within a quantitative dataset. Complementarily, inferential statistical data analysis is intended to "… test hypotheses and generalize results to the population as whole" (Center for Innovation in Research and Teaching, 2018: Online).

### 8.3.1 Descriptive statistical data analysis

Descriptive statistical data analysis, in accordance with the Center for Innovation in Research and Teaching (2018: Online), summarises data and explores patterns within this data through a variety of ways, mainly:
- **Frequencies**: The number of times a particular score or value is found in the data set.
- **Percentages**: Proportion of the count to the sample.
- **Mean**: The numerical average of the sum of counts.
- **Median**: The numerical midpoint of the scores or values that is at the centre of the distribution of the scores.
- **Mode**: The most common score or value for a particular variable.
- **Minimum and maximum values (also referred to as range)**: the highest and lowest values or scores for any variable.

Source: *Center for Innovation in Research and Teaching (2018: Online)*

Descriptive data analysis usually makes use of visual representations patterns (also visualisation) through the use of visual aids such as graphs, histograms, charts and tables, which are very useful in the simplicity with which they summarise complex, sometimes onerous, data. Below is an outline of examples of descriptive data visualisation.

*Table 8.4: Example of a frequency table*

| Ethnicity | Number of children | Percentage of children |
|---|---|---|
| Black African | 30 | 7.71 |
| Black Caribbean | 45 | 11.57 |
| White British | 98 | 25.19 |
| White European | 79 | 20.31 |
| Asian | 65 | 16.71 |
| Biracial | 50 | 12.85 |
| Other | 22 | 5.66 |
| **TOTAL** | 389 | 100 |

*Figure 8.9: Example of a bar graph*

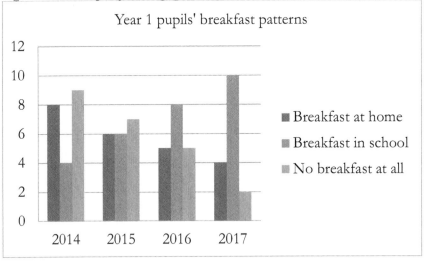

116

*Figure 8.10: Example of a pie chart*

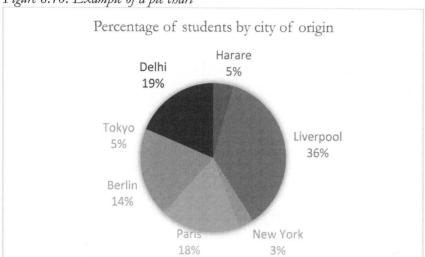

When writing commentary on descriptive statistics, you do not have to highlight every statistic in the visualisation. Rather, only select what you consider interesting and show or explain why it is of interest for that particular dataset. This could be due to a variety of reasons. For examples, the number could be much lower or much higher than expected. Alternatively, it could be because the score is the highest or the lowest on a given variable. Whichever you identify as an interesting outcome, give reasons why it is particularly so.

## 8.3.2 Inferential statistical analysis

Similar to descriptive statistical analysis, there is a range of inferential statistics available for use in quantitative data analysis. The Center for Innovation in Research and Teaching (2018: Online) identifies the three most commonly used:

- **Correlation analysis**: Aids in the examination of the nature of relationship between variables, e.g. the relationship between pupil age and school readiness. The relationship can be strong or weak, positive or negative. Positive correlation is whereby one variable goes in the same direction as the other (Gabi, 2015), e.g. as school age increases, school readiness improves. Conversely, negative correlation is whereby one variable goes in the opposite direction to the other (Gabi, 2015), e.g. as school age increases, school readiness decreases.

- **Analysis of variance (ANOVA)**: Tests "…whether or not the means of two sampled groups is statistically significant or due to random chance. For example, the test scores of two groups of students are examined and proven to be significantly different. The ANOVA will tell you if the difference is significant, but it does not speculate regarding "why"…" (The Center for Innovation in Research and Teaching, 2018: Online).

- **Regression analysis:** Used "…to examine the predictive relationship between identified variables" (Gabi, 2015: 140). For example, to test the question: Does age predict a child's likelihood to experience mental health problems? Please note, however, that it is not possible to use regression analysis to infer causality mainly because other factors will not have been controlled for.

It is, nonetheless, important to note that inferential statistics cannot be conducted with small samples. However, there is a general lack of consensus in the literature on how big a sample should be before inferential statistical analyses can be undertaken (Jones and Bright, 2001) and outcomes are generalisable to the population (Gabi, 2015). That said, the consensus is that – with inferential statistics – the bigger the sample size, the better. The main reason why it is difficult to be prescriptive about ideal sample sizes is that there is a variety of determinants of what an ideal sample size would be for a given study. Binu, Mayya and Dhar (2014) specify six determinants of sample size decisions:
- primary objective of the study
- the type of outcome variable
- study design used
- the statistical analysis planned
- number of groups in the study
- sampling technique to be adopted

As such, we will not prescribe a sample size in this book as much will depend on the position of your study on these six, or even more, points. Consulting your dissertation supervisor would be best as they will take your research context against the six determinants into consideration.

## 8.4 Integrative analysis

Integrative analysis is used in mixed-methods design with the intention to integrate or combine two initially different, separately conducted analyses. So, initially, you conduct qualitative and quantitative data analyses separately. Because both analyses are part of the same study, there is then need to unify the analyses to confirm, corroborate, extend and compare (if there are any differences between qualitative and quantitative analyses on the same point). There is no point calling a design mixed-methods if, in the end, the separate analyses will remain separate. Integrative analysis is, therefore, an opportunity to undertake method triangulation. You may want to look at what each dataset says in relation to each research question and what insights may be drawn from integrating the findings. Table 8.5 below is provided to give your ideas on how you may approach integrative analysis if you adopt the mixed-methods approach.

*Table 8.5: Integrative analysis example*

| Theme (based on research questions) | Quantitative evidence | Qualitative evidence | Integrative interpretation/ Commentary |
|---|---|---|---|
| Stress level | Stress level (m=6.6, SD=3.2) **Note:** Stress scale was 1 (very low) to 10 (very high) | Grace: "My stress levels never stay the same. They fluctuate by term, by class, by workload etc." | xyz |
| Coping strategies | Frequency of direct action coping (m=4.5, SD=4.3). **Note:** Frequency scale was 1 (very rarely) to 5 (very frequently). | David: "Of course, I do switch off. But then (…) switching off doesn't solve the problem (…) so I prefer to deal with the issue, and then I know it's done." | xyz |

## 8.5 Presenting your findings

This is an important stage which requires careful consideration where you think about your paradigmatic position and what this might mean in relation to how you present your findings. Here, you will need to be systematic:

**First** provide a brief description of the context of your research as this will help bring your data to life. If your study was conducted in a school, you may want to say something briefly about the catchment area. What you include here should be relevant to your study and help set the scene. If your participant is a social worker, a brief description of their gender, ethnicity and years in service will help your reader visualise and understand your interpretation of the data. You will then need to **discuss** all key findings drawing on your chosen theoretical standpoints to interrogate the data. It is important to think about how your findings help you answer your research questions. **Next,** systematically give meaning to each finding. **Then,** discuss why you believe these findings are significant. Also explain some of the ways in which your key findings contribute to the ongoing dialogue within the field. **Organisation** is important in findings presentation and analysis. This could be by research question or chronologically, depending on the nature of your study. Whatever way you choose to present your findings, ensure there is cohesion between and across different paragraphs. Table 8.6 below provides examples of how to explain the significance of your findings.

*Table 8.6: Example of how you may present your findings*

- This finding is significant because …
- The significance of this finding lies in that it …
- This result is quite interesting primarily because …
- As much as this finding was unexpected, it carries much importance due to …
- Analysis of findings indicates that this result is unique in three ways. First, it … Second, it … Additionally, it implies …
- The most important educationally relevant finding was …
- In the current study, comparing X with Y showed that …

## 8.5.1 Relating the findings to similar studies

It is important to relate your findings to similar studies you explored in the literature review chapter bearing in mind that every research focus has been studied before. In this section link your findings to results from previous studies that influenced yours and consider aspects of your findings that are similar to previous research and how they relate to or differ from them and in what way. Grounding your findings in existing studies helps support your claims about the importance/ significance of your study whilst at the same time explaining why, in the context of other studies, your findings are still important.

*Table 8.7: Example of how you may relate your findings to those in similar studies*

- These results further support the idea of …
- The finding confirms the association between …
- This is in   line with results from previous studies, for example Gabi (2015) who found that …
- These results are in agreement with those obtained by Smith (2016) which indicated that …
- This supports previous research, such as Knight (2014), into school readiness which links poverty to low reading skills.
- This study has been unable to demonstrate that …
- This outcome is contrary to that of Hughes et al. (2001) who found …
- In contrast to earlier findings, however, no evidence of X was detected.

## 8.5.2 Consider alternative explanations of the findings

You research to find out not to prove. There are multiple explanations of your findings. You will need to judiciously consider all possible explanations of your findings. That means interrogating the data. Do not force the data to say what it does not say. Do not try too hard to prove. Rather than saying, "I know …", ask, "What are the findings telling me?" and is there another way to look at this data? Learn from the results. Do not impose your thoughts on the findings. Consider examples in table 8.8 below.

*Table 8.8: Alternative explanation of findings*

- There are several possible explanations for this result...
- Another possible explanation for this is that ...
- These relationships may partly be explained by ...
- There are, however, other possible explanations.
- It seems possible that these results are due to ...
- This rather contradictory result may be due to ...
- It is difficult to explain this result, but it might be related to ...
- The possible interference of X cannot be ruled out.

## 8.6 Interpretation questionability

Interpretation questionability primarily emanates from exaggeration, overgeneralisation or underreporting findings. To minimise, or even avoid, interpretation questionability, your interpretation must be supportable with evidence. Table 8.9 below provides hints on what you need to be cautious about when interpreting your findings.

*Table 8.9: Interpretation questionability examples*

**Example 1**
**Finding: Children taking part in outdoor play were happy**
1. Does this mean outdoor play causes happiness among children?
2. Or are children playing outside because they are happy?
3. Or, mere coincidence. Children playing outside happen to be happy. No causal link.
4. Is it the outdoor play itself, or is it who they are with that makes these children happy?
5. Could this be just the open space itself and not the playing per se that makes these children happy?
6. Or maybe it is just taking a break from the indoor routine - a break with routine?
7. What evidence do you have for choosing one interpretation?

**Example 2**
**Finding: Pupil stress levels rise during exams**
1. Does this mean exams are causing pupil stress?
2. Could this be just a mere coincidence?

3. Could this be because of how the teachers are managing the exams process, not the exams themselves?

4. Could this not be just the pressure the teachers are exerting on pupils, not the exams themselves per se?

5. Could this be because the teachers have poorly prepared the pupils and, therefore, pupils are stressed because they are inadequately prepared?

6. Out of many alternatives, what evidence would you use for singling out one explanation?

*Table 8.10: Minimising interpretation questionability*

1. Pre-empt the interpretation scepticism during:
   - Instrument design
   - Data collection
2. If there appear to be links between themes, verify with the participants.
3. Probe and follow up, e.g.
   - "Could there be other reasons for this?"
   - "Is this how you consistently feel during this time"
   - "What is it about exams that makes you feel this way? Are there any other factors?"
4. Collect data across different times/ different environments

## 8.7 Writing the conclusion

The conclusion provides a summary of key findings and the extent to which these have answered you research questions. It is important to note that you should not restate all results or introduce new findings in the discussion. Focus your discussion on the findings you have already outlined. In instances where the research was conducted in your own setting, you will need to reflexively explore how this influences your interpretation of the subject. The conclusion should be written in an academically compelling way as this section highlights the significance of your study. Avoid being overly wordy. Rather, write to communicate not to complicate. You will then need to state the limitations of your study and put forward suggestions for further research.

## 8.7.1 Acknowledge the study's limitations

Every study has its own limitations. Acknowledging your own study's limitations does not mean weakening the significance of your study. Do not leave the marker to identify the limitations. Otherwise you will lose marks. Probe. What does your study not do? Which aspects are limited?

*Table 8.11: The limitations of your study could be any of these:*

**1. Methodological**
- e.g. Different methodologies to be considered?

**2. Sample size**
- Too small to make generalisations?

**3. Scope of study**
- Too narrow? Too broad?

**4. Research focus**
- Fuzzy?
- Too broad?
- Too narrow?

*Table 8.12: Examples of how you could state the limitations of your study.*

- These findings may be somewhat limited by …
- These findings cannot be extrapolated to all children because …
- These results must be interpreted with caution because …
- In observational studies, there is a potential for bias from …
- It is important to bear in mind the possible bias in these responses.
- Although exclusion was not a statistically significant predictor of school readiness …, these results should be interpreted with caution. First, …
- However, with a small sample size, caution must be applied, as the findings might not be …

## 8.7.2 Put forward recommendations for further research

Suggestions for further research are often discussed in the same paragraph(s) with the research limitations. After stating the limitations for study, you will then put forward suggestions that will address the identified limitations in order to extend your study. These suggestions could be:

- To use a different methodology
- To find out results from a different sample
- To compare/ corroborate findings
- To further empirical/ academic dialogue on the topic

*Table 8.13: Some examples of how you may put forward further research recommendations*

- This is an important issue for future research.
- Research questions that could be asked include ...
- There are still many unanswered questions about ...
- Several questions remain unanswered at present.
- Despite these promising results, questions remain.
- Further work is required to establish the viability of...
- Further research should be undertaken to investigate the ...
- There is abundant room for further progress in determining ...
- A further study with more focus on X is therefore suggested.
- Future studies on the current topic are therefore recommended.
- To develop a full picture of X, additional studies will be needed that ...
- In future investigations, it might be possible to use a different X in which ...
- Further studies, which take these variables into account, will need to be undertaken.

## 8.8 Self-reflexivity

This is an important stage which requires careful consideration where you think about your paradigmatic position and what this might mean in relation to how you present your findings. Your paradigmatic positioning aids your reader's understanding of the way(s) you are approaching study. Research paradigms are often discussed in the methods and methodology chapter in a detailed way. But you will also need to consider this in your data analysis. Your paradigm frames the way you conduct your research, analyse, make meaning of and write-up your study. We explored the main research paradigms in the previous chapter. It is important to bear in mind that researchers affect and are affected by their research in complex ways. This includes some of the ways in which your identity, experiences, knowledge, values and beliefs influence your interpretations. You will, therefore, need to reflexively explore transactional influences on your perceptions of the subject and meaning-making processes. Being reflexive as an ethical approach to research involves constantly asking yourself why you are choosing to see and make sense of your data in this/these way(s). That means your write-up becomes a process of re-examining, re-considering and re-contextualising your field work experiences. Cannella and Lincoln (2007) cited in Gabi (2013:97) put forward useful questions you may find helpful to consider;

> Whose knowledge is this? Why (as a researcher) do I choose to construct this problem? What assumptions are hidden within my research practices? How could this work produce exclusions? What do I do as I encounter those unexpected exclusions or oppressions that result from the work? What is my privilege (or power position) in this research? How am I subtly re-inscribing my own universals and/or discrediting others?

Your conclusion needs to acknowledge these transactions 'rather than seeing such influences as potential *contamination of the data* to be avoided' (Attia and Edge, 2017:35). Reflexivity allows you to be conscious of your own feelings, emotions, values and beliefs that you bring to your research and how these aid or influence your interpretation of the data.

## 8.9 Summary

The purpose of this chapter was to examine some of the main data analysis approaches, that is discourse analysis, content analysis, thematic analysis – for qualitative research, and descriptive and inferential statistical analyses – for quantitative research – and how these approaches might be used in making sense of the data. Regarding qualitative data analysis, we explored data reduction and the generation of categories to help determine key themes emerging from the data that will then form headings for your analysis chapter. A discussion of the importance of practising self-reflexivity has been provided, which is an acknowledgement of the baggage researchers bring to research which then shapes assumptions about the subject whilst influencing the conduct of and approach to the study. We, therefore, discussed the importance of considering researcher's influences on data collection, analysis, interpretation and write up processes as this tends to be embodied and constituted in power. We also considered quantitative data analysis methods and methodologies – principally descriptive and inferential statistical analyses. In the next chapter, we explore ways in which you can then go on to discuss your findings.

# 9 DISCUSSING FINDINGS AND USING EVIDENCE

## 9.1 Overview

After data analysis, it is important that you highlight the significance of your key findings in the broad context of existing literature. Data analysis isolates key findings for in-depth scrutiny; Discussion of findings contextualises these results within existing literature – both of which steps are important in a dissertation. Data analysis initiates an argument for the significance of the findings; Discussion closes this argument.

According to Annesley (2010), a good discussion of findings achieves two critical goals: interpreting and describing the significance of findings in light of existing literature on the research topic and explaining new insights emerging from the research findings. In this chapter, therefore, we will elucidate and provide guidance on these broad characteristics of an ideal discussion of results.

## 9.2 Interpreting the significance of findings

When interpreting the significance of your findings, perhaps the most important thing to bear in mind is that it is an *interpretation*. You are drawing meaning from what you have identified as key findings of your research. While there are many ways to approach this task, we believe it is best to follow a logical, sequential process like this one:

- Step 1: Outline
- Step 2: Justify

- Step 3: Explain
- Step 4: Close

### 9.2.1 Outline

Having analysed your findings, it is important to make it clear to the reader which, among these findings, are major. **Outlining** them, even as a list, is a good way of informing the reader early on. This also helps you focus your thoughts on what specifically your discussion will be based on. At this stage, it is also helpful to note how you will expand on each of these findings. This is why steps 2 to 3 of the discussion process will be a good aid.

### 9.2.2 Justify

It is not enough to just state what your key findings are and then move on to interpreting them. After outlining, it is key that you **justify** your identification of these results as significant. Your reader needs to know why they are significant. Additionally, it is an opportunity for you to demonstrate you are aware of the reasons why the selected results are important. There are many possible reasons behind selected results being significant. Some of these could be confirmation of initial hypotheses, rejection of hypotheses and extension of what is known. If you had formulated your hypotheses, that is your guess of what will likely be the outcomes of your study, you will be able to determine which of these hypotheses are confirmed and which are not. Another category of findings are those which neither confirm nor contradict but, rather, add to your initial hypotheses. These are results which you may not have formulated hypotheses on, but are still significant in what they add to the topic you researched on. The table below provides an example of how these three dimensions can be covered in your discussion.

*Table 9.1: Justifying the significance of your findings*

**Confirmation of initial hypothesis**
- This result/ These results is/are significant because it/ they confirm the study's hypothesis that ...
- The importance of this result/ these results is primarily due to its/ their confirmation of ...
- The fact that this finding/ these findings are confirmatory of the hypothesis that ... makes it/ them significant.

**Rejection of hypothesis**
- On this result/ these results, the hypothesis that ... is rejected. This makes this/ these result(s) significant.
- Initially, it had been hypothesised that ... would have a negative impact on .... This/ These finding(s) is/ are inconsistent with this hypothesis, which is a significant outcome.
- The hypothesis that ... has a negative impact on ... is rejected because this study has found that .... This is a significant result.

**Extension of what is known**
- This/ These result(s) add(s) to expected outcomes because ... , which is significant.
- When hypotheses of this study were formulated, this/ these result(s) was/ were not taken into account, but is/ are important because ...
- This/ These result(s) is/ are an extension of this research's hypothesis in that it/ they adds to the understanding of the link between ... and ..., which is significant.

### 9.2.3 Explain

A further important step of the results discussion process is **explanation**. While there is some explanation in the justification step, most of it is done at this stage. Here, you should put the significant results in the context of what is already known on the aspects of the topic you researched. Considering the following points would be a good idea:

- In what way are the results similar to what other researchers have found?
- In what way are these findings different to other researchers' findings?
- What do your findings add to what is in the literature to enhance people's understanding of the topic you researched?
- In what aspects of the topic does your study not do that well and, therefore, requires further research?

The table below provides examples of how you can approach the explanation aspect.

*Table 9.2: Explaining results in the context of existing literature*

**How the results are similar to what other researchers have found**

- This/ These result(s) is/ are similar to what other researchers have found on the topic. For example, Reagan (2017) found that …
- This/ These finding(s) is/ are consistent with Smith's (2015) observations that … is a positive contributor to …
- Five years ago, Rogers (2013) found that …, which is in keeping with the result of the present study indicating that …, also …

**How these findings are different to other researchers' findings**

- This/ These result(s) contrast with what other researchers (e.g. Roberts, 2016 and Gabi, 2014) found in relation to … A possible reason for this difference could primarily be that …
- This/ These finding(s) vary from previous results (e.g. Coventry, 2014, Johnson, 2016 and Foster, 2018) who all found that … tends to lead to increased experiences of … This might be due to …
- This is divergent from Jones' (2017) finding that …. The reason for this divergence is possibly …

**What the findings add to what is in the literature**

- This/ These finding(s) complement previous work on the topic (e.g. Blair, 2013 and Forrester, 2006) who found that there is link between ... and .... This study has now found that this link is likely to be ...

- This/ These result(s) contributes to the topic in that it extends existing understanding on ..., which, according to key authors in the area (e.g. Burke, 2018), has been very limited so far.

- The result, signifying the role of ... in people's choices of ... is a further development of Brown's (2015) and Moyo's (2017) ideas on possible causal connection between ... and ...

**Limitations of the study**

- It is important, however, to note that this study does not quite show why ... has such an important role in ... It would be worth conducting further research on the explanation of this relationship.

- Insofar as the extent this is an issue on the population, it is recommended that a large-scale study building on the present work is conducted.

- It would be of much academic interest to carry out a similar study using the mixed methods approach to deepen understanding of ...

- The effect of ... on ... is, however, inconclusively proven by this study. Therefore, further research on this aspect would be of much benefit.

## 9.2.4 Close

For every significant result you discuss, it is helpful to close. A sound interpretation of a result will likely have offered multiple angles from which to make sense of that finding or given competing explanations to a finding, as shown above. It makes sense, therefore, to then state the implication of these multiple interpretations of a finding. It could be an implication to practice, to the field of study or to the body of knowledge on the subject. Consistently closing each significant finding discussed assists in transition or flow between points raised, a necessary enhancement of writing fluency. Here are some examples.

*Table 9.3: Closing discussion of every significant finding*

**Implication to practice**
- In keeping with these multiple explanations, therefore, this might be evidence for why there is a lack of consistency in approaches to coping with ….
- These divergent explanations point to the inconclusive nature of ….
- The pluralistic nature of these alternative observations explains, in part, the differences in approaches to ….

**Implication to the field of study**
- The competing arguments on this finding is indicative of the contrasting, and complementary, schools of thought in the study of …
- The existence of such alternative explanations on this factor opens up new possibilities for further exploration of … in the general study of ….
- In the context of the study on … , it these multiple perspectives on … present a plausible argument for further examination of context-related effects of … on ….

**Implication to the body of knowledge on the subject**
- Insofar as the subject of … is concerned, therefore, these explanations further expand understanding on how outcomes on … will vary according to context.
- These extrapolations extend Banda's (1999) conceptualisation of the role of … on ….
- Collectively, these possible standpoints extend Mabasa's (2003) list on the probable reasons why children experiencing … end up disadvantaged in later life.

## 9.3 Describing the significance of findings

As much as it is good academic practice to outline the significant findings of your study, there is even greater need to go further by stating why the results you identify are significant and in what way. Perhaps one of the biggest challenges of discussion of findings is how to identify what is significant in a multitude of data which is sometimes, if not most of the time, unstructured. If analysis has been done effectively, some structure should be discernible by the time you get to the discussion stage. Identifying significance, then, especially in qualitative data, can be based on a range of points. During analysis, you will have identified dominant, recurrent patterns on aspects of your study's aims or research questions. Alongside this, you could also consider how strongly these patterns address your research questions and aims. Another dimension of significance could be on the strength of relationship with previous similar studies on the topic. This might be how strongly they confirm, contrast with or extend what other studies found on the same topic or subject. This helps locate your own findings in the broader context of the literature which your emerging work will become a part of. Added to this, there is the practice dimension to the identification of what is significant. In a similar way to academic significance, practice significance considers the strength of the research's potential contribution to practice. This could be that, if implemented, the results will lead to a significant change to current practice on the subject or topic dealt with by your research. Alternatively, it might be that the implementation of the identified significant findings of your study would potentially lead to a strong enhancement or improvement of current practice. Table 9.4 below summarises these dimensions of significance.

*Table 9.4: Dimensions of significance shaping the description of findings*

**Dominant, recurrent patterns**
- Explain the nature of the dominant, recurrent patterns in your data.
- This will be in relation to your research questions or research aims.
- Explain why, on the basis of the data, they are recurrent and dominant.
- Explain how strongly these patterns address your research questions and aims.
- If you have adopted the mixed-methods approach significance can be determined by recurrence, or similarity, across the datasets.

**Strength of relationship with similar previous studies on the topic**
- How strongly do the findings confirm what other studies found on the same topic or subject?
- How strongly do the results contrast with what other studies found on the same topic or subject?
- How strongly do your findings extend what other studies found on the same topic or subject?

**Strength of significance to practice**
- Strength of the research's potential contribution to practice.
- Possibly, if implemented, results will lead to a significant change to current practice.
- Findings will result in strong enhancement or improvement of current practice.

## 9.4 Explaining new insights

At the end of the discussion of findings, it is essential to state your conclusions. These are drawn from the key points you will have raised in the chapter, that is what you consider to be the highlights of the chapter. New insights are a result of the synthesis of various key findings emerging from the data analysis and discussion. By synthesis we mean the bringing together or combining of results and establishing what they mean in the broad context in an academic and practice sense and coming up with new ideas. If possible, you could subcategorise this into academic insights and practice insights.

It is essential to state why these emerging insights are of particular interest in both an academic and practice sense. Go back to your research questions and establish if how they are answered could give some new insights regarding what is known on the topic or subject. Alternatively, the findings probably show a new or better way of explaining a concept. It could be even that the results indicate a new solution to an existing problem. Moreover, the results might provide some answers, or significant hints of answers, to an existing problem. The table below gives examples of how you may word your explanation of new insights.

*Table 9.5: Explaining new insights*

**Showing a new or better way of explaining a concept**
- Results emerging from this study further enhance the understanding of ... in the context of ..., which has up to now shown to be a challenge.
- Findings of this study provide a unique understanding of why ... seems to be particularly prevalent among children aged between ... and ....
- Findings on the source of ... within education settings draw us closer to finding a possible explanation of causality.

**Highlighting a new solution to an existing problem**
- Understanding the effectiveness of coping strategies of teachers in this sample brings us closer to finding possible ways of addressing stress among secondary school teachers.
- On the basis of these emerging results, it makes sense to infer that one plausible way of reducing the prevalence of ... among ... could be ....
- In keeping with the finding that ... who are doing well in this setting usually use ... approaches, it appears workload among university students could be effectively managed by ....

**Providing some answers, or significant hints of answers, to an existing problem**

- As indicated in the literature review, researchers (e.g. Wright, 2005 and Moutinho, 2009), have consistently been intrigued by a lack of compelling evidence of an answer to the occurrence of ... among. This finding appears to offer initial hints to the possibility of ... being related to ....

- In the past, educationists have agonised of the scantiness of evidence showing what is the best way to address the school readiness problem. In a small way, these results indicate that best practice shown by case study schools in this research potentially provide a blueprint for future government strategy in the area.

- Consistent with results from the study, particularly the significance of ... to reducing ..., there is a strong suggestion that ... has been persistent due to ....

## 9.5 Summary

Interpreting and describing the significance of findings in the discussion of findings chapter or section of your dissertation should be carried out rigorously and systematically. It principally involves synthesis of results and drawing new insights in light of existing literature on the research topic or subject. This is one of the opportunities which exist for you to make some claims on your contribution to knowledge. This can be confirmation, contradiction or extension of what is known on the topic or subject you researched on. To summarise what you should do in the discussion of findings, Azar (2006) proposes that you provide context; demonstrate why your results are important using the evidence gathered, and supporting it with existing literature; emphasise the positives of your study without exaggerating and closing with an outlook of the future in relation with the topic you studied. In the following chapter we provide guidance on writing the implications chapter or section of your dissertation.

# 10 IMPLICATIONS FOR PRACTICE, RECOMMENDATIONS FOR FURTHER RESEARCH AND CONCLUSIONS

## 10.1 Overview

Implications for practice refer to the influence your research findings are projected to have on a specified professional area or context. Recommendations put forward informed suggestions for further research. Conclusions restate aims, highlight key findings, put forward recommendations and attempt to predict the future outlook of the topic. This chapter takes you through the process of writing a conclusion for your dissertation. It provides examples of useful phrases that will help you write an effective conclusion.

## 10.2 Purpose of the final chapter

The purpose of the concluding chapter in a dissertation is to bring together key insights from your study whilst giving a sense of 'closure' by offering tentative concluding remarks. Avoid introducing new ideas that are not discussed in your dissertation. An effective conclusion begins by restating the focus of your study and why your study is important. Your conclusion should be linked to your introduction without necessarily repeating what you included in your dissertation introduction. You may begin by stating that:

> This study focused on XYZ mainly because it is a key contemporary area of interest in the sector. Thus, there were personal, academic and professional bases for choosing this topic. Personally, xyz. Whilst studies in the field tended to focus on XYZ, this study was approached

139

from .... This was based on the view that .... There were also professional reasons for undertaking this study, namely xyz.

*Table 10.1: Restatement of purpose/ aim – some examples*

This study set out to …
This paper has argued that …
This study has discussed the reasons for …
In this investigation, the aim was to assess …
The aim of the present research was to examine …
The purpose of the current study was to determine …
The main goal of the current study was to determine …
This project was undertaken to design … and evaluate …
The present study was designed to determine the effect of …
The second aim of this study was to investigate the effects of …

After restating your personal, professional and/ or academic justification for your study, you will then need to highlight key aspects of your research findings and how this enabled you to make sense of your study. For example:

This study utilised the mixed-methods design. Adopting the pragmatist paradigm, the research comprised sequential explanatory quantitative and qualitative research methods and methodologies. Questionnaires were first deployed and results thereof analysed. These results then informed follow-up interviews, which were subsequently analysed using thematic analysis. Both datasets were then subjected to integrative analyses and interpreted in accordance with Creswell (2005).

*Table 10.2: Summary of key findings*

This study has identified ...
This study has shown that ...
The research has also shown that ...
The second major finding was that ...
This study has found that generally ...
The investigation of XYZ has shown that ...
The results of this investigation show that ...
The most obvious finding to emerge from this study is that ...
The relevance of XYZ is clearly supported by the current findings.
One of the more significant findings to emerge from this study is
that ...

*Table 10.3: Possible explanations of findings*

In general, therefore, it seems that ...
The results of this study indicate that ...
These findings suggest that in general ...
The findings of this study suggest that ...
Taken together, these results suggest that ...
An implication of this is the possibility that ...
The evidence from this study suggests that ...
Overall, this study strengthens the idea that ...

It is important to provide a section on the limitations of your study. While you are discussing limitations of your study, it is also important to consider the contribution that your study makes to practice and to current research in the field. Please see table 10.4 below.

*Table 10.4: Examples of how to write on contribution to knowledge and limitations*

**Contribution to knowledge, policy or practice**

The finding that ... extends understanding of ...

These results are significant in that they will help in the development of policy on ...

The case study in this research illustrating good practice regarding ... will help settings devise user-friendly ...

**Limitations**

These findings are limited in their implications because ...

Owing to the smallness of the sample, it is difficult to generalise the findings to ...

However, caution needs to be exercised in the use of some of these results as the study was conducted during a particularly difficult time for the setting, immediately after ... had happened.

## 10.3 Being reflexive

Conducting research impacts on you as the researcher in complex ways. In keeping, Jootun, McGhee and Marland (2009) propose that researchers make explicit their relationship between and their influence on the participants. Reay (2007: 611) acknowledges the significance of practising self-reflexivity in the research process and that it is about 'giving as full and honest an account of the research process as possible, in particular explicating the position of the researcher in relation to the research'. Think about the impact of research on the researcher and the impact of the researcher on the research. This is about some of the ways in which your research has impacted on you and how you have impacted on the research.

*Table 10.5: Questions to consider*

- In what ways has the dissertation process changed you as a researcher?
- What could have been done differently?
- What role will this research process have on you as a reflective practitioner?
- What have you learned about the part that research has to play in the life of a reflective practitioner?
- What has this experience taught you about the research process?

## 10.4 Implications of findings to understanding of the subject

Bourner and Greenfield (2016:11) suggest that you think about what the implications of your results are for our understanding of the subject by considering the following possibilities:

*Table 10.6: Implications of findings*

1. You may have filled a gap in the literature.
2. You may have produced a solution to an identified problem in the field.
3. Your results may challenge accepted ideas in the field (some earlier statements in the literature may seem less plausible in light of your findings).
4. Your work may help to clarify and specify the precise areas in which existing ideas apply and where they do not apply (it may help you to identify domains of application of those ideas)
5. Your results may suggest a synthesis of existing ideas.
6. You may provide a new perspective on existing ideas in the field.
7. Your results may suggest new ideas, perhaps new lines of investigation.
8. You may have generated some new questions in the field.

> 9. Your work may suggest new methods for researching your topic.

This will then help you to provide recommendations for further research in your field. Examples provided below will help you begin the recommendations section:

*Table 10.7: Recommendations for further research*

> There is, therefore, a need for...
> Greater efforts are needed to ensure ...
> Provision of ...will enhance ...and reduce ...
> Another important practical implication is that ...
> Moreover, more ... should be made available to ...
> Unless settings adopt ..., ... will not be attained.
> These findings suggest several courses of action for ...

## 10.5 Summary

This chapter explored some of the ways in which a dissertation concluding chapter may be written. Primarily, we looked at implications for practice, recommendations and conclusions. We provided guidance on how you may approach the task of writing about the influence your research will likely have on policy and practice. Furthermore, we considered ways in which you can write about limitations of your findings. To enhance clarity, examples of phrases to use in framing your concluding chapter were provided. In closing, the following short chapter gives you some hints on your abstract and appendices.

# 11 THE ABSTRACT AND APPENDICES

## 11.1 Overview

Besides the main content, there are two further critical parts expected in the dissertation, namely the abstract and appendices. The abstract, although bound within the dissertation, should provide sufficient enough information about the work as a standalone component. On the other hand, appendices form additional accompanying material backing up the core arguments presented in the dissertation, but not necessarily always directly cited. This short chapter seeks to guide you through how to write an effective abstract and key considerations for compiling effective appendices. First, it defines an abstract and then moves on to consider its main features. The next section considers what appendices are, their purpose and composition. The conclusion highlights the key points about the abstract and appendices.

## 11.2 The abstract

An abstract is a concise, self-contained single-paragraph summary of the research which mainly comprises the main themes of the work, "background or initial hypothesis, keywords or subject terms used in the literature review, methodology used, results and findings, and the conclusions or recommendations drawn by the authors" (Imperial College London, 2018: online). In agreement, the Institute of Education Sciences (2018) outlines core elements of an effective abstract which are helpful to consider – purpose, methods, results, implications and additional information. Please see table 11.1 below for supporting information on these elements.

*Table 11.1: Core elements of an effective abstract*

**Purpose**
- Hypothesis and objectives of the study.
- State what the study aimed to achieve.
- What was/ were the aim(s)?

**Methods**
- Key components of the research design.
- Details of sample size, geographic location, demographics, sampling technique(s) and data collection procedures.

**Results**
- Key findings of the study

**Implications**
- Key takeaways
- Links to policy and practice
- Possible future recommended studies to build on the present work

**Additional information**
- List of key terms of the work

## 11.3 Appendices

The appendices section of your dissertation should contain supplementary evidence or data to support main arguments put forward and key points raised in the dissertation. This can be data, tables and figures too complex or too cumbersome to include in the main document (the University of Nottingham, 2018). Table 11.2 below has some of the main data and documentation you may include in your appendices.

*Table 11.2: Suggestions of what may be included in the appendices*

**Data collection instruments**
- Interview transcripts
- Field notes
- Questionnaires
- Complex datasets

**Brief material referred to throughout your dissertation**
- Legislation
- Anonymised setting policies
- Brief background information, e.g. a description or an illustration of your study's theoretical framework

**Evidence of compliance with ethics protocols**
- Anonymised access letters
- Anonymised informed consent forms
- Anonymised ethics forms
- Evidence of study-specific information given to participants

## 11.4 Summary

Although seemingly the simplest of the dissertation endeavour, abstracts and appendices are an important component of your dissertation. The abstract is the first opportunity through which your reader will learn about key features of your study, including purpose, methods, results, implications and additional information. However, it must be brief and in a single paragraph not longer than 300 words. Check with your supervisor or institution dissertation presentation policy for actual wordage of your course dissertation. Appendices, on the other hand contain supplementary material in support of key arguments being put forward in your dissertation such as data collection instruments, brief material referred to throughout your dissertation and evidence of compliance with ethics protocols.

# GLOSSARY

**Abstract**
An abstract is a concise, self-contained single-paragraph summary of the research which mainly comprises the main themes of the work, "background or initial hypothesis, keywords or subject terms used in the literature review, methodology used, results and findings, and the conclusions or recommendations drawn by the authors" (Imperial College London, 2018: online). Usually, this is presented in a single paragraph of between 100 and 300 words.

**Access**
Access refers to the process of ethically asking for, and being granted, permission to carry out your research with specified participants in a targeted setting. Depending on context, access can ethically either be granted by the intended participants themselves or via a gatekeeper.

**Access letter**
An access letter is a written, usually formal, request for permission to carry out specified research in a specified setting for a specified length of time at specified intervals with a specified sample. This permission must be informed – that is, it must be based on sufficiently truthful information, including research topic, aims and methodologies, you will have provided to the gatekeeper or participant about the research.

**Appendices**
Appendices contain supplementary evidence or data to support main arguments put forward and points raised in the dissertation. This can

be the research questionnaire, interview transcripts, anonymised access letters and anonymised consent forms.

## Anonymising

Anonymising is a deliberate act of protecting identities of individuals and settings. This is done by either using pseudonyms or masking identities, e.g. blacking out individual or setting identifiers.

## Active listening

Also known as empathic listening, active listening relates to a researcher's attempt to demonstrate, particularly in interviews or focus groups, good faith unbiased acceptance by a researcher of a participant's experience (Weger, Castle and Emmet, 2010). In interviews or focus groups it is important that, as a researcher, you try to understand the participant's own understanding of the experience they are talking about rather than interpreting it according to your own understanding or biases (Ibid).

## Bias

Bias is researcher's partiality or prejudice in their approach to a study at any stage of the research lifecycle. Smith and Noble (2017) identify five types of research bias, four of which are relevant to this book. These are design bias, selection/ participant bias, data collection bias, measurement bias and analysis bias. Design bias emanates from inconsistencies between different aspects of the design of the research. Selection/participant bias occurs when researcher personal preferences influence the selection of participants for a particular study in an attempt to influence the eventual outcome. Data collection bias and measurement bias happen when a researcher's pre-conceptions influence how the data is collected (Ibid). Analysis bias relates to instances where the investigator selectively analyses data, choosing only that which confirms their own beliefs or personal experiences, "… overlooking data inconsistent with personal beliefs" (Smith and Noble, 2017: 101).

## Closed-ended questions

Closed-ended questions "provide respondents with a fixed number of responses from which to choose an answer" (Lavrakas, 2008: online). These are a common feature in questionnaire surveys.

## Confidentiality

Confidentiality is the conscious protection of participants' identities with the express purpose to protect them from harm, such as victimisation or bullying, that may result in if their identities were disclosed.

## Confirmability

Confirmability is "the degree to which the findings of the research study could be confirmed by other researchers" (Korstjens and Moser, 2017: 121 ) and are clearly supported by the data.

## Credibility

Credibility has to do with whether the research findings are a true representation of reflection of "… participants' original data and is a correct interpretation of the participants' original views" (Korstjens and Moser, 2017: 121 ).

## Data analysis

Data analysis is the systematic process of making sense of the data using a specified analysis framework, establishing patterns and links across the dataset(s), interpreting these links and patterns and drawing contextualised insights.

## Data collection

Data collection is the process of gathering primary data using specific methods, following appropriate methodology and using appropriate data collection instruments.

## Dependability

Dependability is the degree to which it can be determined "…whether the findings of an inquiry would be consistently repeated if the inquiry were replicated with the same (or similar) subjects (respondents) in the same (or similar) context" (Guba, 1981:80).

## Discussion

The purpose of a discussion of findings is to "…interpret and describe the significance of your findings in light of what was already known about the research problem being investigated, and to explain any new understanding or insights about the problem after you've taken the findings into consideration" (Annesley, 2010: online).

## Dissertation supervisor
A dissertation supervisor is an academic member of staff responsible for advising and guiding a student on the research process during the lifecycle of the dissertation research.

## Double-barrelled questions
"A double-barrelled question asks about more than one construct in a single survey question" (Lavrakas, 2008: online). This then makes it difficult, or impossible even, to interpret the response as it will be unclear which part of the question the answer relates to.

## Epistemology
Epistemology refers to what you know, how you come to know it and how valid it is (Koro-Ljungberg, Yendol-Hoppey, Smith and Hayes, 2009).

## Ethics
Ethics are rules, standards and principles governing the conduct and dissemination of research; principally safety, access and consent, confidentiality, voice and empowerment, conflict, participation and integrity.

## Field notes
Field notes are taken during the process of gathering qualitative data "...to facilitate critical reflection when engaging in fieldwork" (Maharaj, 2016: 114).

## Follow-up questions
Follow-up questions are asked to probe or gain a deeper understanding of, or clarification on, a particular subject of discussion in an interview (Camfield, 2014).

## Gatekeeper
In research, a gatekeeper "...stands between the data collector and a potential respondent..." (Lavrakas, 2008: online). Gatekeepers are,

therefore, key to a researcher gaining access to the respondent or research setting.

## Generalisability
Generalisability is the extent to which findings from your research can validly be applied to other contexts than where the study was conducted (Hultsch et al, 2002).

## Hypothesis
A hypothesis is a clear statement of prediction of what the outcome of the intended research is likely to be.

## Implications
Implications of research findings refer to the impact a study is likely to have on policy and practice.

## Instrumentation
Instrumentation refers to "…tools or means by which investigators attempt to measure variables or items of interest in the data-collection process" (Salkind, 2010: online).

## Integrative analysis
Integrative analysis is an analysis process which examines more than one dataset for patterns within and between them and consistencies and inconsistencies.

## Interview schedule
An interview schedule is a list of carefully framed questions to be asked in an interview. These ought to be consistent with research aims and research questions.

## Investigator triangulation
Investigator triangulation is the process of comparing and discussing separately and independently obtained findings between more than one researchers who are involved in the same study

## Leading questions
Leading questions are the types of questions asked in such a way that they influence the respondent towards giving a certain answer.

## Literature review
A literature review explores and discusses key literature in an area your dissertation seeks to examine. This provides research context to your dissertation.

## Method triangulation
Method triangulation involves use of more than one research method with the purpose of collecting data complementing each other whereby weaknesses of one method are offset by strengths of the other.

## Mixed-methods
In mixed-methods designs, quantitative and qualitative methods are used in conjunction within the same study.

## Population
A research population is the overall group from which a collection of respondents participating in the same research project, for which they have met criteria for participation, has been drawn.

## Open-ended questions
Open-ended questions are a type of questions which give respondents the freedom to answer how they wish to express themselves. There is no fixed set of predetermined list of options to choose from.

## Ontology
Ontology has to do with **what** it is that constitutes reality (Scotland, 2012).

## Power relations
Power relations in research refer to the authority the researcher has relative to that of their participants. In the context of their research, the researcher has authority on the direction their study follows, how long it takes and what it involves. This authority can either positively or negatively influence the research process.

## Questionnaire
A questionnaire is a research instrument with a list of questions and measurements for the purpose of collecting data of a specific research

topic to address specific research questions. This instrument tends to be anonymously and independently self-administered.

## Recommendations for further/ future research

Recommendations for further/ future research are a set of suggestions for what needs to be examined further in light of findings of a study. This is usually on the basis of areas which the study has either insufficiently or inconclusively investigated.

## Reliability

Reliability is the capacity of an instrument to result in consistent results (Phelan and Wren, 2005).

## Research design

A research design is the structure and functionality of the study. It concerns itself with the research plan, including the plan's different components and how well or consistently they work together as part of one research process. In practice this is primarily the research approach, methods and methodologies and instrumentation.

## Research focus

Research focus is where a study's emphasis is primarily on, the most important subject at the centre of the study. This tends to be related to the research aim and topic.

## Research instruments

Research instruments are tools with which data is gathered in a study, for example questionnaires, interview schedules etc.

## Research methodology

The research methodology is the **process**, that is **how** a research technique is implemented or put to use.

## Research methods

The research method is the data collection technique used such as interviews, observations, focus groups and questionnaire surveys.

**Research paradigm**
Research paradigms are knowledge influences underpinning one's perspectives and interpretations of phenomena.

**Research plan/ Research proposal**
A research plan/ research proposal is a concise and coherent overview of a research project which specifies the principal issues or questions to be addressed. It identifies the general area of study within which the "…research falls, referring to the current state of knowledge and any recent debates on the topic" and demonstrates the significance of the proposed study (The University of Birmingham, 2018: online).

**Research question**
A research question is a statement of what you hope your study to find an answer or answers to. Some authors distinguish between a research question and a research topic while others use the terms interchangeably. In the former, you can have both a research topic and a list of research questions whose answers the research wishes to investigate.

**Research topic**
A research topic is a title or label which is given to a research project. This label tends to be descriptive to enable readers to easily identify the project.

**Rigour**
Research rigour refers to the soundness and integrity of a research project in terms of its validity and reliability or – in the context of qualitative research – in terms of its credibility, transferability, dependability and confirmability.

**Sample**
A sample refers to a collection of people or participants drawn from the broader population for purposes of research. It is a portion of the population.

**Sampling technique/ strategy**
A sampling technique/ strategy is the approach adopted to select a portion of the population to participate in a study. Examples are

random sampling, opportunity/ convenience sampling and quota sampling.

## Sensitive questions
Sensitive questions are penetrating, complex and delicate and, therefore, require care and caution if they are to be asked in research. If care is not exercised, such questions usually provoke emotional or angry reactions.

## Theme
A research theme is the recurring or dominant idea in/ of a research project.

## Thematic analysis
Thematic analysis is a close examination of, and drawing of plausible inferences from, recurring or dominant ideas from qualitative data.

## Theoretical framework
A theoretical framework is a structure of theories (or a theory) underpinning a study for purposes of explaining, predicting and understanding phenomena and, usually, challenging and extending existing knowledge (Abend, 2008 and Swanson, 2013).

## Theory triangulation
Theory triangulation (also known as theoretical triangulation) is the use of more than one theory to interpret and make sense of the data.

## Transferability
Transferability refers to the extent to which "…the results of qualitative research can be transferred to other contexts or settings with other respondents" (Korstjens and Moser, 2017: 121 ).

## Triangulation
Triangulation as an approach, "…originates in the field of navigation where a location is determined by using the angles from two known points" (Heale and Forbes, 2013: 98). In research, it refers to the reliance on more than one reference point to make sense of phenomena. Key types of triangulation are method, investigator/ observer and theory triangulation.

## Trustworthiness

Trustworthiness is the degree to which findings of a study can be relied on, particularly the research's credibility; transferability, dependability and confirmability.

## Validity

Validity is the capacity of an instrument to measure what it is intended to measure, with particular emphasis on the extent to which results of a study represent what was studied (Phelan and Wren, 2005).

# REFERENCES

Abend, G. (2008) The Meaning of Theory. *Sociological Theory*, 26, 173-199.

Agresti, A. and Finlay, B. (1997) Statistical Methods for the Social Sciences. New Jersey: Pearson Education.

Anderson, E. (2015) Feminist Epistemology and Philosophy of Science. Stanford: Stanford University.

Annesley, T.M. (2010) The Discussion Section: Your Closing Argument. *Clinical Chemistry*, 56, 171-174.

Azar, B. (2006) Discussing your Findings. Washington DC: American Psychological Association.

Baghramian, M. (2015) Relativism. Stanford: Stanford University.

Ball, C. (2009) What Is Transparency? *Public Integrity*, 11 (4), 293-308.

Binu, V.S.; Mayya, S.S. and Dhar, M. (2014) Some basic aspects of statistical methods and sample size determination in health science research. *An International Quarterly Journal of Research in Ayurveda*, 35, 119-123.

Bourdeau, M. (2018) Auguste Comte. Stanford: Stanford University.

Bourner, T. and Greenfield, S. (2016) The Research Journey: Four Steps to Success. In T. Bourner and S. Greenfield (Eds) Research Methods for Postgraduates. Sussex: Wiley.

Camfield L. (2014) Follow-Up Questions. In: Michalos A.C. (eds) Encyclopedia of Quality of Life and Well-Being Research. Springer, Dordrecht.

Creswell, J. W. (2005) Research Design: Qualitative, Quantitative, and Mixed Methods Approaches. London: Sage.

Creswell, J.W. (2013) Steps in Conducting a Scholarly Mixed Methods Study. Discipline-Based Education Research. Lincoln: University of Nebraska.

Creswell, J.W. and Plano Clark, V.L. (2007) Designing and Conducting Mixed Methods Research. Thousand Oaks: Sage.

Dewey, J. (1925) Experience and Nature. Whitefish: Kessinger.

Feilzer, M.Y. (2010) Doing Mixed Methods Research Pragmatically: Implications for the Rediscovery of Pragmatism as a Research Paradigm. *Journal of Mixed Methods Research*, 4, 6-16.

Gabi, C. (2006) Coping Strategies of a Stress-Resilient Teacher. Manchester, The University of Manchester. Master of Science.

Gabi, C. (2015) Person, Process, Context, Time: A Bioecological Perspective on Teacher Stress and Resilience, The University of Manchester. Doctor of Philosophy.

Gabi, J. (2013) Rhizomatic Cartographies of Belonging in Early Years in the UK. Manchester Metropolitan University. Doctor of Philosophy.

Guba, E.G. and Lincoln, Y.S. (1994) Competing paradigms in qualitative research. In N. K. Denzin & Y. S. Lincoln (Eds.), The handbook of qualitative research (pp. 105–117). Thousand Oaks: Sage.

Guba, E.G. (1981) Criteria for assessing the trustworthiness of naturalistic inquiries. *Educational Technology Research and Development*, 29, 75-91.

Heale, R. and Forbes, D. (2013) Understanding triangulation in research. *Evidence Based Nursing*, 16, 1-1.

https://cirt.gcu.edu/research/developmentresources/research_ready/quantresearch/analyze_data [Analyzing Quantitative Research] [Accessed 29/09/2018].

https://eric.ed.gov/?abstract [Guidance on Writing Abstracts] [Accessed 25/09/2018].

https://www.birmingham.ac.uk/schools/law/courses/research/research-proposal.aspx [How to Write a Research Proposal] [Accessed 26/09/2018].

https://research.hud.ac.uk/research-subjects/human-health/template-analysis/example-1/initial-coding/ [Sample transcript and initial coding ] [Accessed 29/09/2018].

http://onlineqda.hud.ac.uk/Intro_QDA/phpechopage_titleOnlineQDA-Examples_QDA.php [Examples of Qualitative Data Analysis (QDA)] [Accessed 29/09/2018].

https://www.imperial.ac.uk/admin-services/library/learning-support/assignment-tips/find-it/abstracts/ [What is an abstract?] [Accessed 25/09/2018].

https://www.nottingham.ac.uk/studentservices/documents/abstractsandappendices.pdf [Abstracts] [Accessed 25/09/2018].

Hultsch, D.F. et al (2002) Sampling and generalisability in developmental research: Comparison of random and convenience samples of older adults. *International Journal of Behavioral Development*, 26, 345-359.

Johnson, R.B. and Onwuegbuzie, A.J. (2004) Mixed methods research: A research paradigm whose time has come. *Educational Researcher*, 33, 14-26.

Jootun, D.; McGhee, G and Marland, G. (2009) Reflexivity: Promoting rigour in qualitative research. *Nursing Standard*, 23, 42-46.

Kivunja, C. and Kuyini, A. B. (2017) Understanding and Applying Research Paradigms in Educational Contexts. *International Journal of Higher Education*, 6, 26-41.

Koro-Ljungberg; M., Yendol-Hoppey, D.; Smith, J.J. and Hayes, S.B. (2009) (E)pistemological Awareness, Instantiation of Methods, and Uninformed Methodological Ambiguity in Qualitative Research Projects. *Educational Researcher*, 38, 687-699.

Korstjens, I and Moser, A. (2017) Trustworthiness and publishing. *European Journal of General Practice*, 24, 120-124.

Lavrakas, P.J. (2008) Closed-Ended Question. Encyclopedia of Survey Research Methods. London: Sage.

Lincoln, Y. S. and Guba, E. G. (1985) Naturalistic Inquiry. Newbury Park: Sage.

Loubert, P.V. (1999) Ethical perspectives in counselling. In Ray, R. & WieseBjornstal, D.M. (eds.), Counseling in Sports Medicine. Leeds: Human Kinetics.

Maharaj, N. (2016) Using field notes to facilitate critical reflection. *International and Multidisciplinary Perspectives*, 17, 114-124.

McNamee, M. and Bridges, D. (2002) The Ethics of Educational Research. Oxford: Blackwell.

Prosser, J. (2008) What constitutes an image-based qualitative methodology? *Visual Sociology*, 11, 25-34.

Reay, D. (2007) Future directions in difference research: Recognizing and responding to difference. In S. N. Hesse-Biber (Ed.) Handbook of feminist research: Theory and praxis. Thousand Oaks: Sage.

Reeves, T. (1994) Managing Effectively: Developing Yourself Through Experience. Oxford: Butterworth-Heinemann.

Robson, C. (2002) Real World Research: A Resource for Social Scientists and Practitioner-researchers (2nd edition). London: Wiley.

Robson, C. and McCartan, K. (2016) Real World Research (4th Edition). London: Wiley.

Rorty, R. (1999) Philosophical and Social Hope. London: Penguin.

Rose, G. (2007) Visual Methodologies. London: Sage.

Rose, G. (2014) On the relation between 'visual research methods' and contemporary visual culture. *Sociological Review*, 62, 24-46.

Rysiew, P. (2016) Epistemic Contextualism. Stanford: Stanford University.

Salkind, N.J. (2010) Instrumentation. In Encyclopedia of Research Design. London: Sage.

Saunders, M.; Lewis, P. and Thornhill, A. (2009) Research Methods for Business Students. Essex: Pearson.

Scotland, J. (2012) Exploring the Philosophical Underpinnings of Research: Relating Ontology and Epistemology to the Methodology and Methods of the Scientific, Interpretive, and Critical Research Paradigms. *English Language Teaching*, 5, 9-16.

Seliger, H. W. and Shohamy, E. (1989) Second Language Research Methods. Oxford: Oxford University Press.

Shacklock, G. and Smyth, J. (1998) Being Reflexive in Critical Educational and Social Research. London: Falmer.

Sheldon, J. (2017) Problematizing Reflexivity, Validity, and Disclosure: Research by People with Disabilities About Disability. *The Quality Report*, 22(4), 984-1000.

Silverman, D. (2017) Doing Qualitative Research. London: Sage.

Smith, J. and Noble, H. (2017) Bias in research. *Evidence Based Nursing*, 17, 100-101.

Swanson, R. A. (2013) Theory Building in Applied Disciplines. San Francisco: Berrett-Koehler Publishers.

Teddlie, C. and Tashakkori, A. (2003) Major Issues and Controversies in the use of Mixed Methods in the Social and Behavioural Sciences, In C. Teddlie and A. Tashakkori (Eds), Handbook of Mixed Methods in Social and Behavioural Research. Thousand Oaks: Sage.

Teddlie, C. and Tashakkori, A. (2006) A General Typology of Research Designs Featuring Mixed Methods. *Research in Schools*, 13, 12-28.

The Social Research Association (2018) A Code of Practice for the Safety of Social Researchers. London: The Social Research Association.

The University of Manchester (2018) *Dissertations: The A-Z of literature reviews*. Manchester: University of Manchester Press.

Weger, H., Castle, G.R. and Emmett, M.C. (2010) Active Listening in Peer Interviews: The Influence of Message Paraphrasing on Perceptions of Listening Skill. *The International Journal of Listening*, 24, 34-49.

Williams, E. and O'Connor, T. (2017) "I have collected qualitative data; now what do I do?" approaches to analysing qualitative data. *Research and Review Insights*, 1, 1-5.

# INDEX

**Abstract**, **2**, **26**, **149**
**Access**
 Access letter, **15**, **94**, **149**
**Active listening**, **150**
**Analysis of variance**
 ANOVA, **118**
**Anonymising**
 anonymity, **150**
**Appendices**, **145**, **146**, **147**, **149**
*Bar graph*, **116**
**Bias**
 Researcher bias, **48**, **150**, **162**
**Censuses**
 census, **63**
**Closed-ended questions**, **150**
complementarity
 complement, **69**
**conclusion**
 concluding, **24**, **38**, **70**, **92**, **123**, **139**, **144**, **145**
**Confidentiality**
 anonymity, **51**, **95**, **151**
**Confirmability**, **84**, **151**
Conflict
 conflicting, **96**
**consent**
 consent letter, **31**, **61**, **92**, **94**, **95**, **96**, **147**, **150**, **152**
**Consistency**, **68**, **82**, **88**
constructionism
 constructionist, **86**
**Constructionism**

social constructionism, **86**
Constructivist
 constructivism, **72**
Content analysis, **107**
contextualism
 contextualist, **86**, **87**
**Contextualism**
 contextualist, 87, 162
**Correlation analysis**
 correlations, **117**
**Credibility**, **84**, **151**
Cultural norms, **87**
*Cyclical approach*, **106**
**Data analysis**
 analysis, **19**, **35**, **78**, **129**, **151**
DATA ANALYSIS
 analysis, **105**
**Data collection**
 data gathering, **17**, **35**, **43**, **81**, **123**, **147**, **150**, **151**
**Dependability**, **84**, **151**
Descriptive statistical data analysis
 descriptive statistics, **115**
diary
 diaries, **44**, **45**, **46**
Discourse analysis, **107**
**Discussion**, **6**, **19**, **54**, **151**, **159**
**Dissertation supervisor**, **152**
**Double-barrelled questions**, **48**, **152**
empiricism

empiricist, **86**

**Empiricism**
empiricist, **87**
epistemology
epistemological, **77**, **85**,
**86**, **87**, **88**, **89**

**Epistemology**, **85**, **152**, **159**,
**162**

**ethics**
ethical, **18**, **23**, **32**, **91**, **92**,
**95**, **98**, **102**, **147**

**Ethics**
ethical, **102**, **152**, **161**

EVIDENCE
data, **129**

**explanations**
explanation, **14**, **20**, **121**,
**122**, **133**, **134**

falsity, **87**

feminist
feminism, **86**, **161**

**Field notes**
field-notes, 147, 152

**Findings**
results, **2**, **3**, **4**, **5**, **6**, **7**, **19**,
**20**, **26**, **31**, **51**, **68**, **77**,
**78**, **79**, **80**, **81**, **85**, **89**,
**102**, **107**, **120**, **121**, **123**,
**124**, **125**, **129**, **130**, **131**,
**132**, **133**, **135**, **136**, **137**,
**138**, **141**, **143**, **144**, **145**,
**146**, **149**, **151**, **152**, **153**,
**155**, **158**

**Follow-up questions**
probe, **46**, **152**

**Frequencies, 115**

**Gatekeeper, 152**

**Generalisability, 153**

hybrid epistemologies
hybrid, **86**

**Hybrid epistemologies**
Hybrid epistemology, **88**

**hypothesis, 130, 131, 145,**
**149, 153**

**Hypothesis, 146, 153**

**Implication**
implications, **134**

**Implications**
implications of findings,
**143**, **146**, **153**

IMPLICATIONS
implication, **139**

Inferential statistical
analysis
inferential statistics, **117**

**insights**
ideas, **2**, **20**, **50**, **129**, **136**,
**137**, **138**, **139**, **151**, **152**

**Instrumentation**
research instruments, **153**,
**162**

Integrative analysis, **119**,
**153**

**Interpretation, 35, 68, 122**

Interpretivism
interpretivist, **86**, **87**

Interpretivist
Interpretivism, **72**

**Interview schedule, 153**

**Investigator triangulation**
observer triangulation, **153**

**Justify**
justification, **78**, **129**, **130**

Knowledge attribution
knowledge, **87**
**Leading questions**, **48**, **153**
**limitations**, **27**, **71**, **81**, **123**,
**124**, **125**, **141**
**Literature review**
review of the literature, **4**,
**38**, **154**
**Mean**
average, **115**
**Method triangulation**
methodology
triangulation, **154**
methodology
methodologies, **13**, **17**, **18**,
**19**, **23**, **29**, **37**, **43**, **46**,
**51**, **55**, **59**, **60**, **62**, **71**,
**81**, **84**, **86**, **125**, **145**,
**149**, **151**, **155**, **161**
methods
research methods, **2**, **3**, **4**,
**5**, **17**, **18**, **19**, **24**, **25**, **26**,
**27**, **29**, **30**, **35**, **43**, **44**,
**55**, **56**, **59**, **62**, **63**, **64**,
**69**, **70**, **78**, **85**, **86**, **87**,
**88**, **89**, **103**, **133**, **136**,
**140**, **144**, **145**, **147**, **151**,
**154**, **155**, **162**
**Objectivism**
objectivist, **86**
ontology
ontological, **77**, **86**, **89**
**Ontology**, **85**, **86**, **154**, **162**
**Open-ended questions**, **154**
Participation
participant, **97**

**patterns**
themes, **5**, **10**, **20**, **108**,
**135**, **136**, **151**, **153**
**Percentages**, **115**
phenomena
phenomenon, **44**, **50**, **56**,
**59**, **70**, **71**, **72**, **86**, **156**,
**157**
*Pie chart*, **117**
**Population**, **154**
Positivism
positivist, **86**, **87**
**Power relations**, **154**
Pragmatism
pragmatist, **86**, **87**, **88**
**problem**
problems, **3**, **26**, **29**, **36**, **38**,
**46**, **137**, **138**, **143**, **151**,
**152**
**purpose**
aim, **1**, **2**, **3**, **24**, **25**, **28**, **32**,
**50**, **52**, **53**, **54**, **79**, **102**,
**139**, **140**, **145**, **147**, **151**,
**154**
Qualitative, **44**, **86**, **87**, **159**,
**161**, **162**
Quantitative, **62**, **71**, **86**, **87**,
**159**
questionability, **122**, **123**
**Questionnaire**, **63**, **154**
Reality
realism, **86**
reasoning, **87**
**recommendations**
recommend, **2**, **6**, **7**, **66**,
**88**, **125**, **144**, **145**, **149**

Recommendations for further/ future research, 155
Regression analysis, **118**
relativism
  relativist, **86**
**Relativism**
  relativist, **87, 159**
Reliability, **82, 84, 155**
research
  investigation, **2, 3, 4, 5, 6, 7, 8, 9, 10, 13, 14, 15, 16, 18, 19, 21, 23, 24, 25, 26, 27, 28, 29, 30, 31, 32, 33, 34, 35, 36, 37, 38, 43, 44, 46, 47, 48, 50, 51, 52, 53, 54, 55, 56, 59, 60, 61, 62, 63, 69, 70, 71, 77, 78, 79, 80, 81, 82, 83, 84, 85, 86, 88, 89, 91, 92, 93, 94, 95, 96, 97, 98, 99, 100, 101, 102, 103, 107, 120, 121, 123, 125, 129, 131, 132, 133, 135, 136, 137, 138, 140, 141, 142, 143, 144, 145, 146, 149, 150, 151, 152, 153, 154, 155, 156, 157, 158, 160, 161, 162, 171**
**Research design, 155**
**Research focus, 124, 155**
**Research instruments**
  instrumentation, **155**
**Research paradigm, 156**
**Research plan**

research proposal, **156**
**Research question, 156**
**research topic**
  research title, 3, 8, 13, 16, 18, 25, 26, 33, 35, 44, 69, 85, 88, 102, 129, 138, 149, 155, 156
**Research topic, 156**
**Rigour**
  research rigour, **156**
**Risk, 93, 94**
**Sample, 81, 124, 156**
**Sampling technique, 156**
Self-reflexivity, **125**
**Sensitive questions, 157**
**significance**
  significant, **25, 29, 30, 33, 34, 44, 59, 61, 69, 120, 121, 123, 129, 131, 135, 136, 138, 142, 151, 156**
social entities, **86**
socially constructed
  social construction, **86**
**Subjectivism**
  subjectivist, **86**
Thematic analysis, **108, 157**
**Theme, 157**
**Theoretical framework**
  conceptual framework, **157**
**Theory triangulation**
  theoretical triangulation, **84, 85, 157**
**Transferability, 84, 157**
**Triangulation, 84, 157**

**Trustworthiness**, **78**, **158**, **161**
Truth, **84**, **87**
*truth* and *reality*
truth, **72**, **73**, **74**

Universalisation
universal, **92**
**Validity**, **77**, **89**, **158**, **162**
Voice and empowerment, **95**

## ABOUT THE AUTHORS

### Dr Controllah Gabi PhD

Dr Controllah Gabi is a Lecturer in Applied Social Sciences and Course Leader at the University Centre, Trafford College Group in the UK. He is also dissertation module leader at the same institution. Dr Controllah Gabi is also a University of Hull External Examiner for Social Sciences BA (Hons) and MA programmes delivered at Doncaster College and a current member of the British Educational Research Association (BERA) UK. He has previously been a member of the American Educational Research Association (AERA). Dr Controllah Gabi's other professional roles include Link Tutor (University of Chester and Sheffield Hallam University, both UK). His professional experience includes Higher Education Coordinator and Programme Leader. Dr Controllah Gabi holds a PhD Education, MSc Educational Research (both from the University of Manchester, UK), BA (Hons) Business and ICT Education (Manchester Metropolitan University, UK); Qualified Teacher Status (General Teaching Council of England, UK); BBA (Azaliah University, USA); Diploma in Primary Education (University of Zimbabwe) and Certificate in Marketing (Institute of Marketing Management, South Africa).

### Dr Josephine Gabi PhD

Dr Josephine Gabi is a Senior Lecturer in Early Years and Childhood Studies at Manchester Metropolitan University, UK. Dr Josephine Gabi holds a PhD Education and Social Research; Master of Research, Education and Society (MRes); MA Higher Education; Postgraduate Certificate in Academic Practice (PGCAP); BA (Hons) Early Childhood Studies (Manchester Met. University); CRA & SEDA Personal Tutoring and Academic Advising Professional Qualification and Personnel Management (IPMZ). Dr Josephine Gabi is also a Fellow of the Higher Education Academy and external examiner at Edgehill University for the BA (Hons) Early Childhood Studies and Sociology programmes. Dr Josephine Gabi's research interests are in theories and methodologies in education and social research particularly post-qualitative methodologies.

Printed in Poland
by Amazon Fulfillment
Poland Sp. z o.o., Wrocław

81513242R00103